Liberalism Divided

1-9-97

Liberalism Divided

Freedom of Speech
and the Many Uses
of State Power

OWEN M. FISS

WestviewPress
A Division of HarperCollins*Publishers*

Chapter 3 previously appeared as Owen M. Fiss, "Silence on the Street Corner," in *Public Values in Constitutional Law*, edited by Stephen Gottlieb (Ann Arbor: The University of Michigan Press, 1993). Copyright © by the University of Michigan 1993. Reprinted by permission of the University of Michigan Press. Chapter 4 previously appeared as Owen M. Fiss, "Freedom and Feminism," 80 *Georgetown Law Journal* 2041 (1992). Reprinted with the permission of the publisher; © 1992 Georgetown University. Chapter 5 is reprinted by permission of The Yale Law Journal Company and Fred B. Rothman & Company from *The Yale Law Journal*, Vol. 100, pages 2087–2106.

Copyright © 1996 by Westview Press, Inc., A Division of HarperCollins Publishers, Inc.

Published in 1996 in the United States of America by Westview Press, Inc., 5500 Central Avenue, Boulder, Colorado 80301-2877, and in the United Kingdom by Westview Press, 12 Hid's Copse Road, Cumnor Hill, Oxford OX2 9JJ

Library of Congress Cataloging-in-Publication Data
Fiss, Owen M.
   Liberalism divided: freedom of speech and the many uses of State
power / Owen M. Fiss.
      p.   cm.
   Includes bibliographical references and index.
   ISBN 0-8133-2484-X (hc). — ISBN 0-8133-2485-8 (pbk.)
   1. Freedom of speech.   I. Title.
JC591.F57   1996
323.44'3—dc20   95-46272
                                                                      CIP

The paper used in this publication meets the requirements of the American National Standard for Permanence of Paper for Printed Library Materials Z39.48-1984.

10   9   8   7   6   5   4   3   2   1

To William J. Brennan, Jr., and Harry Kalven, Jr.,
for their enduring lessons on liberty

Contents

Liberalism Divided

Introduction

Liberals are at war with themselves. For some time, freedom of speech has held them together, but now it is a source of division and conflict.

During the 1950s, at the height of the Cold War, political forces tried to use the state apparatus to protect the nation from subversion and the threat of communism. The Communist Party of the United States and its leaders were criminally prosecuted and countless citizens linked to the Party were fired from government jobs—not for any overt act against the state but simply for the advocacy of ideas at odds with the established social order. Liberals denounced such exercises of state power and used the First Amendment and its guarantee of free speech for that purpose. They insisted that the fears that fueled these coercive measures were greatly exaggerated and that these measures threatened to silence forceful criticism of the status quo.

In the 1960s, liberals were again united under the banner of free speech. This time they opposed the efforts of many southern states and localities to suppress the civil rights movement and the many searing protests and demonstrations to which it gave rise. Liberals complained, almost in unison, that state power was being used to quell public criticism and was therefore at odds with the protection of free speech provided in the First Amendment. In taking this stance, they drew upon liberal political theory and its brief on behalf of individual rights and the ideal of the limited state.

Over the last twenty-five years, the First Amendment agenda has changed and the liberal consensus has been shattered. Admittedly, some of the traditional controversies have persisted, and on these issues liberals have held together. One such controversy centers around the Pentagon Papers case of 1971, discussed in Chapter 7 of this book. In that case, the Nixon administration sought to stop the leading newspapers of the country from publishing a classified study of the American effort in Vietnam, and liberals joined together in applauding the Supreme Court's decision to resist such censorship. Such moments of unity during the seventies and eighties were, however, the exception. For the most part, liberals have been deeply divided over the free speech controversies that gave that era its distinctive character. These are the controversies that have most engaged my attention in recent years and that are the principal subject of the essays collected in this volume.

One of the most salient free speech controversies of the recent period revolves around the legislative program to place limits on expenditures for political campaigns. Another consists of the effort of political activists to use the power of the state to gain access to the shopping centers of the country for the purpose of promoting their ideas. These arenas are privately owned, but have become the public squares of contemporary America. The 1970s and 1980s were also marked by bitter disputes over the effort to regulate the press, not for purposes of restricting its coverage, as in the Pentagon Papers case, but rather to enhance the diversity of viewpoints presented to the public. Political activists sought access to the mass media and insisted that state agencies regulate the media to allow for the presentation of opposing viewpoints.

All of these cases raised questions in my mind as to the proper relationship of economic and political power and the role the First Amendment might play in structuring that relationship. The first three chapters—"Free Speech and Social Structure," "Why the State?" and "Silence on the Street Corner"—speak to that question and map the shifts in Supreme Court doctrine in this period. The last chapter—"Building a Free Press"—starts with the revolutions of 1989 in Europe and examines the impact economic power might have on free speech in the context of a society undergoing a transition from dictatorship to democracy.

Inequalities of power may have a social rather than an economic basis, and in recent years liberals have divided over the effort to account for such differences in free speech doctrine. One area of conflict has been pornography. During the late 1950s and 1960s, the Supreme Court fashioned a constitutional definition of "obscenity" in order to place limits on state regulation of sexually explicit material. Only books, magazines, and films that met this narrow definition could be proscribed. While conservatives fought for the right of the state to protect traditional sexual mores and decried the Supreme Court's stance, liberals uniformly embraced the effort of the Warren Court to curb the censorship of pornography and viewed the sexual politics of the late 1960s as an important source of personal and political freedom.

During the late 1970s and early 1980s, however, feminists—long a vital component of the liberal coalition—launched a new campaign against pornography, and as a result this area of the law became another contested domain of liberalism. The new campaign against pornography differed from those of the past in that the proposed regulation was intended not to preserve traditional mores concerning sexuality but rather to enhance equality for women. As discussed in more detail in my essay "Freedom and Feminism" (Chapter 4), a number of the leaders of the feminist movement claimed that pornography eroticizes the domination of women and transforms women into sexual objects to be used by men and thus is partially responsible for their subordination in domains both private and public.

A similar concern about the impact that public utterances may have upon the social status of disadvantaged groups has recently led to a revival of interest in regulation of what is called "hate speech," though the psychological dynamic by which that speech inflicts its harm differs from that of pornography and the group allegedly victimized is not primarily women but racial and religious minorities. The permissibility of regulating hate speech is explored in Chapter 6, which takes as its point of departure the famous 1992 Supreme Court decision in *R.A.V. v. St. Paul, Minnesota.* As with pornography, the question posed is whether the regulation of hate speech is consistent with freedom of speech. On this issue, liberals once again find themselves drawn into sharp combat.

Liberals have also become divided over the programs of the modern state that subsidize speech activities. In the 1970s and early 1980s, the core problem related to the purchase of books for public schools and their libraries; today it is funding for the arts and public television. Liberals have traditionally viewed the First Amendment as creating a shield around the individual citizen, protecting the citizen from state interference, but such an understanding of free speech becomes increasingly unhelpful when the state acts in an allocative rather than a regulatory manner. By necessity, allocative programs contemplate continuous interaction between state and citizen and require the state to choose among competing ideas.

Some liberals have responded to this dilemma by insisting that the state withdraw from the field altogether and stop subsidizing speech. They argue that subsidization is inconsistent with the duty of the state to be neutral among differing viewpoints. Others have resisted such a retrenchment, pointing to the contribution that state-supported libraries and public schools, for example, have long made to our public life and political freedom. State subsidization, they argue, liberates speech and culture from a strict dependence on the market. But even this group is sharply divided within itself over the appropriate constitutional standards for judicial supervision of these allocative programs. How might state neutrality be maintained in this sphere? This issue is explored in Chapter 5, "State Activism and State Censorship," which I wrote in response to the controversy that erupted in 1989 and 1990 over the decision of the National Endowment for the Arts to fund an exhibition of Robert Mapplethorpe's photographs.

The division within liberal circles prompted by the free speech controversies of the 1970s and 1980s is in part attributable to the maturation of liberalism as a political philosophy. Whereas liberalism in the nineteenth century was defined almost exclusively by the defense of individual liberty against state intrusion, today its mandate is more pluralistic. Contemporary liberalism, at least as practiced in the United States, is as devoted to furthering equality as it is to protecting liberty.

In the legal domain, this ideological shift can be traced to the Civil War Amendments of the 1860s that abolished slavery and promised all citizens the equal protection of the laws. Of even greater significance might be the Supreme Court's decision in *Brown v. Board of Education* in the mid-1950s and the revolution in American law that it spurred. *Brown* transformed the constitutional order and its governing political philosophy, claiming a place for equality as central as that for liberty.

In academic circles, the change in liberalism can be seen most clearly in the work of John Rawls, the preeminent political philosopher of our day. In *A Theory of Justice* (1971), Rawls made many important contributions to liberal theory, but perhaps his most distinctive contribution was the articulation and defense of what he referred to as "the difference principle." This principle called for redistribution in favor of the worst-off social group and, in so doing, introduced a strong egalitarian element into the liberal creed. In the work of other leading liberal theorists such as Ronald Dworkin (*Taking Rights Seriously* (1977) and *A Matter of Principle* (1985)), Thomas Nagel (*Equality and Partiality* (1991)), and Bruce Ackerman (*Social Justice and the Liberal State* (1980)), the commitment to equality took other forms but was no less manifest.

Equality has thus become one of the defining goals of liberalism. As a result, the traditional commitment of liberal theory to state minimalism necessarily has become compromised. The limited state may be an instrument for furthering liberty, but, as many recognized, the pursuit of egalitarian objectives often requires strong exercises of state power, including curbs on speech or expressive activity. Those who support the regulation of pornography and hate speech, for example, have insisted that sometimes liberty must be sacrificed in order to protect disadvantaged groups from social stigmatization and subordination. Similar egalitarian sentiments inform the debates over campaign finance, access to shopping centers, regulation of mass media, and state subsidies for art, education, or libraries. The purpose of such state activity is to give the economically disadvantaged speech opportunities roughly comparable to those enjoyed by the rich. This intervention is defended by many liberals as a proper pursuit of egalitarianism even though it entails the sacrifice of individual liberty, specifically the freedom to decide how to deploy one's property or other economic resources to further political goals.

Formulated in these terms, the free speech controversy of the last two decades can be analyzed as one confronting liberals with a choice between transcendent values. Which shall be given priority, liberty or equality? Such a conflict is familiar in the history of political thought and even in the constitutional domain. For that reason, the present moment in the history of freedom of speech may be understood as nothing more than a transference of a familiar dilemma to a new realm. But I see within contemporary free speech controversies another problem, the exploration of which might be taken as the overarching and unifying theme of this collection. I see within these controversies not simply a conflict between liberty and equality but also, and perhaps more fundamental, a conflict between liberty and liberty. The division within liberalism arises not from its pluralistic commitments and inability to prioritize equality and liberty but rather, I maintain, from a dispute over the very meaning of freedom. What is at issue is two different ways of understanding liberty.

Some liberals see freedom of speech as protecting the individual interest in self-expression or the right of the individual to say whatever he or she wishes. For them, the state is *the* threat against which the individual must be protected. Others understand freedom in more social terms. According to this account, the role of the First Amendment is to preserve the fullness and openness of public debate: to make certain that the people are aware of all the issues before them and the arguments on both sides of these issues. Free speech, in this view, is a public right—an instrument of collective self-determination—and the state is presented in a new guise, possibly as a friend of freedom. Admittedly, the state may interfere with the robustness of public debate, but there is no reason to presume that it will do so, and we are invited to imagine that the state might act in a way that actually furthers the cause of freedom.

Campaign finance poses one example. Some liberals defend state regulation in order to make certain that the voices of the rich do not drown out those of the less privileged. The concern is not simply with equalizing the opportunities of the less affluent—putting them on an equal footing with the rich—but with the impact such disparities have on the quality of public discourse. A similar point can be made about the other free speech controversies that so divide liberals. Aside from the impact on the social status of disadvantaged groups such as women or minorities, some liberals support the regulation of pornography and hate speech on the hypothesis that these forms of expression silence disadvantaged groups and thus distort public debate. State regulation of private centers of power—say, shopping centers or the mass media—is advocated as a way of presenting the public with information from diverse, even antagonistic, sources. State subsidies for broadcasting or the arts are supported as a way of freeing speech from a strict dependence on the market, which certainly is not neutral in its impact on speech and cannot be counted upon to provide citizens with all they must know in order to exercise their sovereign prerogative.

Liberal support for state interventions of the nature just outlined depends on contested empirical judgments—for example, about the silencing effect of pornography or the market's distortions of public debate. It also assumes that the state apparatus will not be captured by the powerful and used in the opposite way from that intended—not to enrich but to impoverish public debate. Disagreement is certainly possible on all these fronts, as I indeed have acknowledged in the essays that follow, but the fierce resistance within some liberal circles to such state intervention strikes me as more ideologically than instrumentally inspired. The state interventions proposed in recent years conflict with the classical liberal demand for state minimalism, but this demand has, in the constitutional domain, been transformed into a private conception of free speech that blindly privileges the self-expressive interest of the individual over the informational needs of the public.

These disagreements have given the free speech debates now raging in the United States a special character and intensity. Not only do they call upon us to confront afresh the familiar conflict between liberty and equality, but even more fundamentally they require us to decide for ourselves what liberty means. These essays, written over the last decade and collected in this volume for the first time, take up this challenge. They are rooted in the constitutional experience of the United States but speak to the question that, of necessity, absorbs every democratic order, East or West, new or old: What is freedom?

1
Free Speech and
Social Structure

PROLOGUE

I began teaching at the University of Chicago in the late 1960s, and I was fortunate enough to develop a close relationship there with one of the leading free speech scholars of the period, Harry Kalven, Jr. See Owen M. Fiss, Kalven's Way, *43* University of Chicago Law Review *4 (1975). In the fall of 1974, just after I moved to Yale, Kalven died and left on his desk a huge manuscript that he had begun only a few years earlier. Jamie Kalven, Harry's son, then began the almost impossible task of readying this manuscript for publication. For the next decade or so, I worked closely with Jamie on the project. See Editor's Note to Harry Kalven, Jr.,* A Worthy Tradition *(1988).*

When the process of editing the Kalven manuscript was nearly complete, I turned to the First Amendment itself and began teaching and writing in the field. I soon grew uneasy with Kalven's celebratory mood toward the then prevailing body of decisions on free speech—a mood that pervaded his book and was aptly captured by its title. I kept wondering why I had such a different reaction to the received tradition. Part of it, I realized, was due to a difference in our dispositions—Harry always saw the best in things. In time, however, I came to the conclusion that our difference arose primarily from the fact that Harry had premised his analysis on a paradigm that struck me as outmoded: the street corner speaker.

In the essay that follows—first presented in November 1985 as the John F. Murray Lecture at the University of Iowa College of Law and published the next year in the Iowa Law Review—*I pursued this thought and proposed that we shift the organizing free speech paradigm from the street corner to CBS. Now, a decade later, I find myself confronting the question whether the CBS paradigm itself has been rendered obsolete by the technological revolution that has carried us into cyberspace. See* In Search of a New Paradigm, *104* Yale Law Journal *1613 (1995).*

F reedom of speech is one of the most remarkable aspects of American constitutional law. It helps define who we are as a nation. The principle is rooted in the text of the Constitution itself, but it has been the decisions of the Supreme Court over the last half century or so that have, in my view, nurtured that principle, given it much of its present shape, and account for much of its energy and sweep. These decisions have given rise to what Harry Kalven called a "free speech tradition."[1]

In speaking of a tradition, Kalven, and before him, Karl Llewellyn[2] and T.S. Eliot[3] (talking about the shoulders of giants), aspired to an all-embracing perspective. Everything should be included—nothing left out, not the dissents, not even the decisions overruled. Every encounter between the Court and the First Amendment is to be included. The tradition is, however, no mere encyclopedia; it has a distinct shape or direction or point. Those who speak of a free speech tradition try to see all the decisions and to abstract from them a shared understanding of what free speech means—what lies at the core and what at the periphery, what lies beyond the protection of the First Amendment and what is included, where the law is headed, etc. The whole has a shape. The shape is not fixed for all time, since each new decision or opinion is included within the tradition and thus contributes to refiguring the meaning of the whole, but the tradition also acts as a constraining force on present and future decisions. The tradition is the background against which every judge writes. It defines the issues; provides the resources by which the judge can confront those issues; and also creates the obstacles that must be surmounted. It orients the judge.

I believe it is useful to view the free speech decisions of the Supreme Court as a tradition, and I am also tempted to celebrate that tradition in much the way that Kalven did. But for me that is only half the story. It also seems to me that the tradition is flawed in some important respects—so much so that it might be necessary to begin again, if that is even possible.

My concerns first arose in the seventies—one of the few periods when America wondered out loud whether capitalism and democracy were compatible. In the political world these doubts were linked to Watergate and the eventual resignation of President Richard Nixon. The precipitating event was the break-in at the Democratic National Headquarters, but by the time the impeachment process had run its course, we realized how thoroughly economic power had begun to corrupt our politics. Congress responded with the Campaign Reform Act of 1974,[4] imposing limits on contributions and expenditures and establishing a scheme for the public funding of elections.

The tension between capitalism and democracy was also a special subject of concern to the academy, as evidenced by the excitement and controversy generated by the publication in 1977 of Charles Edward Lindblom's book *Politics and Markets*.[5] Lindblom tried to show that, contrary to classical democratic theory, politics was not an autonomous sphere of activity, but was indeed shaped and controlled by the dominant economic interests it was supposed to regulate. As a consequence of this "circularity," the most important issues of economic and social structure—what Lindblom called the "grand issues"—remained at the margins of politics. Voters were not actually considering the continued viability of capitalism, the justness of market distributions, or the structure within which organized labor was allowed to act because, Lindblom argued, of the control exercised by corporate interests over the political agenda.[6]

While academics were reading and debating Lindblom's book, and while politicians were trying to make sense of Watergate, the Supreme Court was faced with a number of free speech cases that required it to examine the relationship of political and economic power. The Court was asked whether it was permissible for a state to extend the fairness doctrine to the print media,[7] and whether the FCC was obliged to provide critics of our efforts in Vietnam access to the TV networks to promote their views.[8] In another case the Campaign Reform Act of 1974 was attacked;[9] and in still another a challenge was raised to a Massachusetts statute limiting corporate expenditures in a referendum on the income tax.[10] Political activists, lacking funds to purchase space or time in the media, sought access to the shopping centers to get their message across to the public, and they also turned to the courts for this purpose.[11] Admittedly, issues of this character had been presented to the Court before, but in the seventies they arose with greater frequency and urgency, and they seemed to dominate the Court's First Amendment docket.

These cases presented the Court with extremely difficult issues, perhaps the most difficult of all First Amendment issues, and thus one would fairly predict divisions. One could also predict some false turns. What startled me, however, was the pattern of decisions: Capitalism almost always won. The Court decided that a statute that granted access to the print media to those who wished to present differing views was invalid; that the FCC did not have to grant access for editorial advertisements in the electronic media; that the political expenditures of the wealthy could not be curbed; and that the owners of the large shopping centers and malls that constitute the civic centers of suburban America need not provide access to pamphleteers. Democracy promises collective self-determination—a freedom to the people to decide their own fate—and presupposes a debate on public issues that is (to use Justice Brennan's now classic formula) "uninhibited, robust, and wide-open."[12] The free speech decisions of the seventies, however, seemed to impoverish rather than enrich public debate and thus threatened one of the essential preconditions for an effective democracy. And they seemed to do so in a rather systematic way.

My first inclination was to see these decisions as part of the program of the Court largely constituted by President Nixon and led by his appointee, Warren Burger, to establish a new priority for liberty and to bring an end to the egalitarian crusade of the Warren Court. The idea was that in these free speech cases, as in the school financing area,[13] the Burger Court was not willing to empower the poor or less advantaged if that meant sacrificing the liberty of anyone. On reflection, however, the problem seemed deeper and more complicated. I saw that at issue was not simply a conflict between equality and liberty, but also, and more importantly, a conflict between two conceptions of liberty. The battle being fought was not just liberty v. equality, but liberty v. liberty, or to put the point another way, not just between the First Amendment and the Equal Protection Clause, but a battle *within* the First Amendment itself. I also came to understand that the Court was not advancing an idiosyncratic conception of liberty, but was in fact working well within the free speech tradition. The Court was not crudely substituting entrepreneurial liberty (or property) for political liberty;[14] the rich or owners of capital in fact won, but only because they had advanced claims of political liberty that easily fit within the received tradition. Money is speech—just as much as is picketing or selling a book.

In time I became convinced that the difficulties the Supreme Court encountered in the free speech cases of the seventies could ultimately be traced to inadequacies in the free speech tradition itself. The problem was the tradition, not the Court. The tradition did not *compel* the results—no body of precedent could. Arguably, there was room for a nimble and determined craftsman working within the tradition to come out differently in one or two of these cases, or maybe in all of them. But, on balance, it seemed that the tradition oriented the Justices in the wrong direction and provided ample basis for those who formed the majority to claim, quite genuinely, that they were protecting free speech when, in fact, they were doing something of a different, far more ambiguous, character. This meant that criticism would have to be directed not simply at the Burger Court but at something larger: at a powerfully entrenched, but finally inadequate body of doctrine.

I

For the most part, the free speech tradition can be understood as a protection of the street corner speaker. An individual mounts a soapbox on a corner in some large city, starts to criticize governmental policy, and then is arrested for breach of the peace. In this setting the First Amendment is conceived of as a shield, as a means of protecting the individual speaker from being silenced by the state.

First Amendment litigation first began to occupy the Supreme Court's attention during World War I, a time when the constitutional shield was rather weak. The street corner speaker could be arrested on the slightest provocation. Those early decisions were openly criticized, most notably in the dissents of Brandeis and Holmes, but that criticism—eloquent and at times heroic—stayed within the established framework and sought only to expand the frontiers of freedom incrementally; it sought to place more restrictions on the policeman and to give more and more protection to the street corner speaker. In this incremental quality, the criticism took on the character of the progressive movement in general, and also shared its fate. The progressive critique achieved its first successes during the thirties, at the hands of the Hughes Court, but its final vindication awaited the Court led by Earl Warren: It was only then that the shield around the speaker became worthy of a democracy.

What largely emerged from this historical process is a rule against content regulation that now stands as the cornerstone of the free speech tradition. The policeman cannot arrest the speaker just because he does not like what is being said. Reasonable time, place, and manner regulations are permitted—the speaker must not stand in the middle of the roadway—but the intervention must not be based on the content of the speech or a desire to favor one set of ideas over another. To be sure, the Court has allowed the policeman to intervene in certain circumstances on the basis of content, as when the speaker is about to incite a mob. But even then the Court has sought to make certain that the policeman intervenes only at the last possible moment, that is, before the mob is unleashed. In fact, for most of this century First Amendment scholarship has largely consisted of a debate over the "clear and present danger" and "incitement" tests, in an effort to find a verbal formula that best identifies that last possible moment.[15] The common assumption of all those who participated in that debate—finally made explicit in the 1969 decision of *Brandenburg v. Ohio*,[16] perhaps the culmination of these debates and in many respects the final utterance of the Warren Court on this subject—is that the policeman should not step in when the speaker is only engaged in the general expression of ideas, however unpopular those ideas may be.[17]

I would be the first to acknowledge that there is something noble and inspiring about the fifty-year journey from the World War I cases[18] to *Brandenburg* in 1969. A body of doctrine that fully protects the street corner speaker is indeed an accomplishment of some note; the battles to secure that protection were hard fought and their outcome far from certain. *Brandenburg* is one of the blessings of our liberty. The problem, however, is that today the street corner has become marginal to public debate, and the doctrinal edifice that seemed to someone like Kalven so glorious with the street corner speaker in mind is largely unresponsive to the conditions of modern society.

Under the tradition extolled by Kalven, the freedom of speech guaranteed by the First Amendment amounts to a protection of autonomy—law places a shield around the speaker. However, the theory that animates this protection, that inspired Kalven[19] and before him Meiklejohn,[20] and that now dominates the field,[21] casts the underlying purpose of the First Amendment in social or political terms: The purpose of free speech is not individual self-actualization, but rather the preservation of democracy, and the right of a people, as a people, to decide what kind of life it wishes to live. Autonomy is protected not because of its intrinsic value, as a Kantian might insist, but rather as a means or instrument of collective self-determination. We allow people to speak so others can vote. Speech allows people to vote intelligently and freely, aware of all the options and in possession of all the relevant information.

The crucial assumption in this theory is that the protection of autonomy will produce a public debate that will be, to use the talismanic phrase once again, "uninhibited, robust, and wide-open." The tradition assumes that by leaving individuals alone, free from the menacing arm of the policeman, a full and fair consideration of all the issues will emerge. The premise is that autonomy will lead to rich public debate. From the perspective of the street corner, that assumption might seem plausible enough. But when our perspective shifts, as I insist it must, from the street corner to, say, CBS, this assumption becomes highly problematic. At that point, autonomy and rich public debate—the two free speech values—might well diverge and become antagonistic.[22] Under CBS, autonomy may be *insufficient* to ensure a rich public debate. Oddly enough, it might even become *destructive* of that goal.

Some acknowledge the shift of paradigms and the obsolescence of the street corner, but would nonetheless view CBS simply as a new version of the old forum—an electronic street corner.[23] They would demand access to the network as though it were but a forum for the expression of views and insist that the right of access to that forum should not follow the incidence of ownership. This view moves us closer to a true understanding of the problem of free speech in modern society, for it reveals how the freedom to speak depends on the resources at one's disposal, and it reminds us that more is required these days than a soapbox, a strong voice, and the talent to hold an audience. On the other hand this view is incomplete: It ignores the fact that CBS is not only a forum but also a speaker, and thus understates the challenge that the shift in paradigms poses to the received tradition. For me CBS is both a forum and a speaker, and it is CBS's status as speaker that renders the tradition most problematic. As speaker, CBS can claim the protection of autonomy held out by the tradition, and yet the exercise of that autonomy might not enrich, but rather impoverish, public debate by limiting the views expressed on the airwaves, and thus frustrate the democratic aspirations of the tradition.

In thinking of CBS as a speaker, and claiming for it the benefit of the tradition, I assume that the autonomy protected by the tradition need not be confined to individuals. It can extend to institutions. Autonomy is not valued by Meiklejohn and his followers because of what it does for a person's development (self-actualization), but rather because of the contribution it makes to our political life, and that contribution can be made by organizations just as much as by individuals. The NAACP, the Nazi Party, CBS, and the First National Bank of Boston are as entitled to the autonomy guaranteed by the tradition as is an individual, and no useful purpose would be served by reducing this idea of institutional autonomy to the autonomy of the various individuals who (at any one point of time) manage or work within the organization.

Implicit in this commitment to protecting institutional autonomy is the understanding that organizations have viewpoints and that these viewpoints are no less worthy of First Amendment protection than those of individuals. An organization's viewpoint is not reducible to the views of any single individual, but is instead the product of a complex interaction between individual personalities, internal organizational structures, the environment in which the organization operates, etc. The viewpoint of an organization such as CBS or First National Bank of Boston might not have as sharp a profile as that of the NAACP or Nazi Party (that is probably one reason why we think of a network as a forum), but that viewpoint is nonetheless real, pervasive, and communicated almost endlessly. It is not confined to the announced "Editorial Message," but extends to the broadcast of *Love Boat* as well. In the ordinary show or commercial a view of the world is projected, which in turn tends to define and order our options and choices.

From this perspective, the protection of CBS's autonomy through the no-content-regulation rule appears as a good. The freedom of CBS to say what it wishes can enrich public debate (understood generously) and thus contribute to the fulfillment of the democratic aspirations of the First Amendment. The trouble, however, is that it can work out the other way too, for when CBS adds something to public debate, something is also taken away. What is said determines what is not said. The decision to fill a prime hour of television with *Love Boat* necessarily entails a decision not to broadcast during the same hour a critique of the President's foreign policy or a documentary on one of Lindblom's "grand issues." We can thus see that the key to fulfilling the ultimate purposes of the First Amendment is not autonomy, which has a most uncertain or double-edged relationship to public debate, but rather the actual effect of a broadcast: On the whole does it enrich public debate? Speech is protected when (and only when) it does, and precisely because it does, not because it is an exercise of autonomy. In fact, at times autonomy might have to be sacrificed to make certain that public debate is sufficiently rich to permit true collective self-determination. What the phrase "the freedom of speech" in the First Amendment refers to is a social state of affairs, not the action of an individual or institution.

The risk posed to freedom of speech by autonomy is not confined to situations when it is exercised by CBS, or by the other media, but occurs whenever speech takes place under conditions of scarcity, that is, whenever the opportunity for communication is limited. In such situations one utterance will necessarily displace another. With the street corner, the element of scarcity tends to be masked; when we think of the street corner we ordinarily assume that every speaker will have his or her turn, and that the attention of the audience is virtually unlimited. Indeed, that is why it is such an appealing story. But in politics, scarcity is the rule rather than the exception. The opportunities for speech tend to be limited, either by the time or space available for communicating or by our capacity to digest or process information. This is clear and obvious in the case of the mass media, which play a decisive role in determining which issues are debated, and how, but it is true in other contexts as well. In a referendum or election, for example, there is every reason to be concerned with the advertising campaign mounted by the rich or powerful, because the resources at their disposal enable them to fill all the available space for public discourse with their message. Playing Muzak on the public address system of a shopping mall fills the minds of those who congregate there. Or consider the purchase of books by a library, or the design of a school curriculum. The decision to acquire one book or to include one course necessarily entails the exclusion of another.

Of course, if we had a clear view of what should be included in the public debate, we would have a firm basis for determining whether the public debate that will result from the exercise of autonomy will permit true collective self-determination. Herbert Marcuse argued, for instance, that advocacy of war, racism, or economic exploitation was antithetical to democratic values and should not be tolerated.[24] Such a substantive baseline makes life easier but it is not essential. Even without it there is every reason to be concerned with the quality of public discourse under a regime of autonomy, for the protection of autonomy will result in a debate that bears the imprint of those forces that dominate the social structure. In the world of Thomas Jefferson, made up of individuals who stand equal to one another, this might not be a matter of great concern, for it can be said that the social structure, as well as the formal political process, is itself democratic. But today we have every reason to be concerned, for we live in a world even further removed from the democracy Jefferson contemplated than it is from the world of the street corner speaker.

The fear I have about the distortion of public debate under a regime of autonomy is not in any way tied to capitalism. It arises whenever social power is distributed unequally: Capitalism just happens to be one among many social systems that distribute power unequally. I also think it wrong, even in a capitalist context, to reduce social power to economic power, and to attribute the skew of public debate wholly to economic factors; bureaucratic structures, personalities, social cleavages, and cultural norms all have a role to play in shaping the character of public debate. But I think it fair to say that in a capitalist society, the protection of autonomy will on the whole produce a public debate that is dominated by those who are economically powerful. The market—even one that operates smoothly and efficiently—does not assure that all relevant views will be heard, but only those that are advocated by the rich, by those who can borrow from others, or by those who can put together a product that will attract sufficient advertisers or subscribers to sustain the enterprise.

CBS is not a monopoly, but competes with a few other networks (and less powerful media) for the public's attention. The fact that CBS's managers are (to some indeterminate degree) governed by market considerations does not in any way lessen the risk that the protection of autonomy—staying the hand of the policeman—will not produce the kind of debate presupposed by democratic theory. The market is itself a structure of constraint that tends to channel, guide, and shape how that autonomy will be exercised. From the perspective of a free and open debate, the choice presented to viewers by the market, between say *Love Boat* and *Fantasy Island,* is trivial. In this respect, CBS and the rest of the broadcast media illustrate, by example, not exception, the condition of all media in a capitalist society. True, CBS and the other networks operate under a license from the government or under conditions of spectrum scarcity. But the dangers I speak of are not confined to such cases, for distortions of public debate arise from economic rather than legal or technical factors.

Individuals might be "free" to start a newspaper in a way that they are not "free" to start a TV station, because in the latter case they need both capital and government approval, while for the newspaper they need only capital. But the need for capital is itself a source of concern and drives a wedge between autonomy and public debate. Licensing may distort the market in some special way, but even the market dreamt of by economists will leave its imprint on public debate, not only on issues that directly affect the continued existence of the market, but on a much wider range of issues from gender equality to nuclear proliferation (though with such issues it is often difficult to predict the shape and direction of the skew). No wonder we tend to identify the free speech tradition with the protection of "the marketplace of ideas."[25]

II

Classical liberalism presupposes a sharp dichotomy between state and citizen. It teaches us to be wary of the state and equates liberty with limited government. The free speech tradition builds on this view of the world when it reduces free speech to autonomy and defines autonomy to mean the absence of government interference. Liberalism's distrust of the state is represented by the antagonism between the policeman and soapbox orator and by the assumption that the policeman is the enemy of speech. Under the received tradition, free speech becomes one strand—perhaps the only one left[26]—of a more general plea for limited government. Its appeal has been greatly enhanced by our historical commitment to liberalism.

In asking that we shift our focus from the street corner to CBS, I do not mean to deny altogether the distinction between state and citizen presupposed by classical liberalism. Rather, my point is more to suggest that we arc not dealing with hermetically sealed spheres. CBS is neither a state actor nor a private citizen but something of both. CBS is privately owned and its employees do not receive their checks directly from the state treasury. It is also true, however, that CBS's central property—the license—has been created and conferred by the government. It gives CBS the right to exclude others from its segment of the airwaves. In addition, CBS draws upon advantages conferred by the state in a more general way, through, for example, the laws of incorporation and taxation. CBS can also be said to perform a public function: education. CBS is thus a composite of the public and private. The same is true of the print media, as it is of all corporations, unions, universities, and political organizations. Today the social world is largely constituted by entities that partake of both the public and private.

A shift from the street corner to CBS compels us to recognize the hybrid character of major social institutions; it begins to break down some of the dichotomies between public and private presupposed by classical liberalism. It also renders pointless the classificatory game of deciding whether CBS is "really" private or "really" public, for the shift invites a reevaluation of the stereotypical roles portrayed in the tradition's little drama. No longer can we identify the policeman with evil and the citizen with good. The state of affairs protected by the First Amendment can just as easily be threatened by a private citizen as by an agency of the state. A corporation operating on private capital can be as much a threat to the richness of public debate as a government agency, for each is subject to constraints that limit what it says or what it will allow others to say. The state has a monopoly on the legitimate use of violence, but this peculiar kind of power is not needed to curb and restrict public debate. A program manager need not arrest someone (lawfully or otherwise) to have this effect, but only choose one program over another, and although that choice is not wholly discretionary or arbitrary, but is constrained by the market, that does not limit the threat that it poses to the integrity of public debate. Rather, it is the source of the problem. All the so-called private media operate within the same structure of constraint, the market, which tends to restrict and confine the issues that are publicly aired.

Just as it is no longer possible to assume that the private sector is all freedom, we can no longer assume that the state is all censorship. That too is one of the lessons of the shift from the street corner orator to CBS. It reminds us that in the modern world the state can enrich as much as it constricts public debate: The state can do this, in part, through the provision of subsidies and other benefits. Here I am thinking not just of the government's role in licensing CBS, but also of government appropriations to public television and radio, public and private universities, public libraries, and public educational systems. These institutions bring before the public issues and perspectives otherwise likely to be ignored or slighted by institutions that are privately owned and constrained by the market. They make an enormous contribution to public discourse, and should enjoy the very same privileges that we afford those institutions that rest on private capital (and, of course, should be subject to the same limitations).

We can also look beyond the provision of subsidies, and consider whether the state might enrich public debate even by regulating in a manner made familiar by the policeman. CBS teaches that this kind of governmental action—once again based on content—might be needed to protect our freedom. The power of the media to decide what they broadcast must be regulated because, as we saw through an understanding of the dynamic of displacement, this power always has a double edge: It subtracts from public debate at the very moment that it adds to it. Similarly, political expenditures might have to be curbed to make certain that the voices of the less affluent are not drowned out. In the past we have ambivalently recognized the value of state regulation of this character on behalf of speech—we have allowed a fairness doctrine for the broadcast media and some regulation of campaign financing. But even these regulatory measures have been forever embattled, and in any event, more, not less, is needed. For example, there should also be laws requiring the owners of the new public arenas—the shopping centers—to allow access for political pamphleteers.

A commitment to rich public debate will allow, and sometimes even require, the state to act in these ways, however repressive they might at first seem. Autonomy will be sacrificed, and content regulation sometimes allowed, but only on the assumption that public debate might be enriched and our capacity for collective self-determination enhanced. The risks of this approach cannot be ignored, and at moments they seem alarming, but we can only begin to evaluate them when we weigh in the balance the hidden costs of an unrestricted regime of autonomy.

III

At the core of my approach is a belief that contemporary social structure is as much an enemy of free speech as is the policeman. Some might move from this premise to an attack upon the social structure itself—concentrations of power should be smashed into atoms and scattered in a way that would have pleased Jefferson. Such an approach proposes a remedy that goes directly to the source of the problem, but surely is beyond our reach, as a social or legal matter, and maybe even as an ethical matter. The First Amendment does not require a revolution. It may require, however, a change in our attitude about the state. We should learn to recognize the state not only as an enemy, but also as a friend of speech; like any social actor, it has the potential to act in both capacities, and, using the enrichment of public debate as the touchstone, we must begin to discriminate between them. When the state acts to enhance the quality of public debate, we should recognize its actions as consistent with the First Amendment. What is more, when on occasions it fails to, we can with confidence demand that the state affirmatively so act. The duty of the state is to preserve the integrity of public debate—in much the same way as a great teacher—not to indoctrinate, not to advance the "Truth," but to safeguard the conditions for true and free collective self-determination. It should constantly act to correct the skew of social structure, if only to make certain that the status quo is embraced because we believe it the best, not because it is the only thing we know or are allowed to know.

A question can be raised whether the (faint-hearted) structural approach I am advocating really represents a break with the free speech tradition, for some traces of a welcoming attitude toward the state can be found within the tradition. One is the *Red Lion* case, which upheld the fairness doctrine and the regulation of content for a speaker such as CBS.[27] This decision does not fit into the overall structure of the tradition taken as a whole, and never has been sufficiently rationalized. It has been something of a freak, excused, but never justified, on the ground that broadcasters are licensed by the government. It has never grown, as an adequately justified precedent might, to allow a state to impose a similar fairness obligation on newspapers or to allow the fairness doctrine and all that it implies to become obligatory rather than just permissible. Its trajectory has been just the opposite. It is of no small significance to me that Kalven (and a number of the other First Amendment scholars working within the tradition) signed briefs in the *Red Lion* case itself on the side of the media.[28]

There is, however, one other aspect of First Amendment doctrine that evinces a welcoming attitude toward the state and that is more firmly entrenched and perhaps more adequately justified. I am now referring to what Kalven called the "heckler's veto."[29] This doctrine has its roots in Justice Black's dissent in *Feiner v. New York,*[30] but it is now an established part of the tradition. It recognizes that when a mob is angered by a speaker and jeopardizes the public order by threatening the speaker, the policeman must act to preserve the opportunity of the individual to speak. As Kalven once put it, the duty of the policeman is to arrest the mob. The doctrine of the heckler's veto, welcoming strong action by the state, might thus appear as an opening wedge for my plea for a reversal of our ordinary assumptions about the state, but one that would allow the Court to work within the tradition. Upon closer inspection, however, this seems to me wishful thinking, and I believe that a more radical break with the past is needed.

First, the heckler's veto does not require an abandonment of the view that free speech is autonomy. State intervention may be necessary in this instance to make the speaker's autonomy "real" or "effective." The person on the soapbox should be given a *real* chance to speak. In contrast, the approach I am advocating is not concerned with the speaker's autonomy, real or effective, but with the quality of public debate. It is listener-oriented. Intervention is based on a desire to enrich public debate, and though the concept of "real" or "effective" autonomy might be so stretched as to embrace the full range of interventions needed to enrich the public debate, the manipulative quality of such a strategy will soon become apparent once the extensiveness and pervasiveness of the intervention is acknowledged. It is also hard to see what is to be gained by such a strategy. Autonomy, in its inflated version, would remain as the key value, but note that while in the received tradition it operated as a response to government intervention, under this strategy it would serve as a justification of such intervention. Autonomy would be nominally saved, but put to a different use.

Second, although the doctrine of the heckler's veto welcomes the strong arm of the law, it does so only on rare occasions, when violence is about to break out, and then only to divert the police action away from the speaker and toward the mob. The general rule is that the state should not intervene, but when it must, it should go after someone other than the speaker. In contrast, the structural approach contemplates state intervention on a much more regular and systematic basis. A prime example of such intervention is, once again, the fairness doctrine, a varied and elaborate set of regulations and institutional arrangements that evolved over several decades. Other instances of this sort of intervention can be found in federal and state laws regulating campaign contributions and expenditures, or in the laws of some states creating access to privately owned shopping centers for political activities. These laws entail a form of state intervention that is more regular and more pervasive than that contemplated by the occasional arrest of the heckler.

Third, when the policeman arrests hecklers, no interests of any great significance seem to be jeopardized. The government is interfering with the hecklers' freedom, but hecklers are not objects of much sympathy. Hecklers are obstructionists, who are not so much conveying an idea as preventing someone else from doing so. They are defined rather two-dimensionally, as persons who refuse to respect the rights of others. Yes, they will have their chance on the soapbox, if that is what they want, but they must wait their turn. The issue appears to be one of timing. But the laws that have divided the Supreme Court over the past decade, and that the structural approach seeks to defend, jeopardize interests that are more substantial than those represented by hecklers.

At the very least, the laws in question involve a compromise of the rights we often believe are attached to private property—the right to exclude people from the land you own, or to use the money you earn in any way that you see fit. In some cases the stakes are even greater: free speech itself. The laws in question threaten the freedom of an individual or institution to say what it wants and to do so precisely because of the content of what is being said. One branch of the fairness doctrine requires a network to cover "public issues," and another requires a "balanced presentation." In either case, a judgment is required by a government agency as to what constitutes a "public issue" and whether the presentation is "balanced." By necessity, attention must be paid to what is being said, and what is not being said. Similarly, laws that regulate political expenditures to prevent the rich from completely dominating debate also require some judgment as to which views have or have not been sufficiently represented. The same is true even if the state acts through affirmative strategies, such as when it grants subsidies to candidates or purchases books or sets a curriculum.

From the perspective of autonomy these dangers are especially acute, and present what some might feel a decisive reason against intervention. Even if we shift the perspective, and rich public debate is substituted for autonomy as the controlling First Amendment value, there is still good reason to be concerned, and to a greater degree than we are when the heckler is silenced. The stated purpose of the government intervention and content regulation might be to enrich debate, but it might have precisely the opposite effect. It might tend to narrow the choices and information available to the public and thus to aggravate the skew of debate caused by the social structure. In fact, there is good reason to suspect that this might be the case, for, as suggested by Lindblom's idea of circularity, the social structure is as likely to leave its imprint on government action (especially of a legislative or administrative character) as it is to leave its mark on the quality of public debate.

IV

Freedom has its costs. The ones I just described are sufficient to distinguish the approach I am advocating from that implicit in the rule against the heckler's veto, and the general tradition of which it is part. But a question still remains—perhaps the ultimate one—whether they are reason enough to reject the structural approach altogether and turn back to the received tradition and the protection of autonomy. Are the costs just too great? When the government intervention requires a sacrifice of what might be regarded as ordinary values, for example, those associated with property rights, then the answer seems clearly "no." Free speech is no luxury. Sacrifices are required, and though there are limits to the sacrifice (as Justice Jackson put it, the Constitution is no "suicide pact"[31]), free speech lies so close to the core of our constitutional structure as to warrant tipping the scales in its favor. In this regard the structuralist can confidently borrow the weighted balancing process used by progressives to protect speech in the interest of autonomy. Traditionally, speech is protected even if it causes inconvenience, a congestion, or a loss of profits, and I see no reason why the same rule could not be applied to further public debate— where the state intervenes as a friend rather than an enemy of speech.

This perspective could help in a number of the cases that stymied the Court in the seventies. A law creating access to a shopping center might interfere with the property rights of the owners, and cause some loss of sales (by keeping away those who do not like to be bothered by politics), but those interests might have to be sacrificed in order to fulfill the democratic aspirations that underlie the First Amendment. To use one of the phrases that inspired the progressives of the fifties and sixties and that gave the tradition much of its vitality, freedom of speech is a "preferred freedom."[32] The only difference is that under the structural approach the enrichment of public debate is substituted for the protection of autonomy and free speech operates as a justification rather than as a limit on state action. The same process of weighted balancing, with the hierarchy of values that it implies, is used, though the traditional perspective on the relationships between the state and freedom is reversed. The notion of "preferred freedoms" or weighted balancing is, however, of little help when the interests sacrificed or threatened by state action are not "ordinary" ones, like convenience or expense, but are also grounded in the First Amendment. Then, so to speak, the First Amendment appears on both sides of the equation: The state may be seeking to enrich public debate but might in fact be impoverishing it.

This danger is presented by the fairness doctrine and that—not the talk about infringement of institutional autonomy—is what makes the doctrine so problematic. The doctrine seeks to enhance public debate by forcing broadcasters to cover public events and to present opposing sides of an issue; but it simultaneously restricts debate by preventing the media from saying what they otherwise might (in response to market pressures, or to advance the political views of the managers or financial sponsors, etc.). The hope is that public debate will be enriched, but the fear is that it might work in the opposite direction, either directly by forcing the networks to cover issues that are not important, or indirectly by discouraging them from taking chances, and by undermining norms of professional independence. Federal and state laws that restrict political expenditures by the rich or corporations also might be counterproductive. These laws seek to enhance public debate by allowing the full range of voices to be heard, including those of the less wealthy. But at the same time these laws might overcorrect, slanting the debate in favor of one view or position, and in that way violate the democratic aspirations of the First Amendment.

I do not believe that this danger of First Amendment counterproductivity arises in every single instance in which the state intervenes to enhance public debate, as is evident from my discussion of the shopping center cases (I put the displacement of Muzak by the songs of protest to one side). Nevertheless, believing as I do that scarcity is the rule rather than the exception in political discourse, and that in such situations one communicative act displaces another, I must acknowledge that this danger of counterproductivity is almost always present. This danger was acknowledged in the discussion distinguishing intervention contemplated by the structuralist and that allowed under the heckler's veto doctrine, and deserves emphasis again, for as Lindblom's analysis of the problem of circularity teaches, the state is not immune to pressures and manipulations. We turn to it because it is the only hope, the only means to correct the distorting influence of social structure on public debate, and yet there is every reason in the world to fear that the state is not as "public" as it appears but is in fact under the control of the very same forces that dominate the social structure. Indeed, I chose CBS (rather than, say, the shopping center) as the new paradigm, and insisted that it be viewed as a speaker (as well as a forum), in order to underscore, rather than to minimize, the problematic character of state intervention. CBS impeaches the received tradition, but also acts as a painful reminder to the structuralist that whenever the state adds to public debate it is also taking something away. The hope against hope is that in the final analysis we will be better off than under a regime of autonomy.

The burden of guarding against the danger of First Amendment counterproductivity will largely fall to the judiciary. Judges are the ultimate guardians of constitutional values, and due to institutional arrangements that govern tenure and salary and due to professional norms that insulate them from politics, they are likely to be more independent of the forces that dominate contemporary social structure (the market) than other government officials. The burden of protecting the First Amendment is theirs, and under the structural approach it is likely to be an excruciating one. Judges are accustomed to weighing conflicting values, but the conflict here is especially troublesome because the values on both sides seem to be of similar import and character.

We cannot casually insist that the courts allow the political agencies to experiment or to take a risk, as we do when something like productive efficiency or administrative convenience is at stake, for the evils to be suffered are qualitatively equal to the benefits to be gained. Nor can we take comfort in doctrines of deference that generally ask courts to respect the prerogatives of legislative or administrative agencies. Those agencies might be as captive of the forces that dominate social structure as is public discourse itself. And I see no more reason in this context than I do in the discrimination area[33] to revert to an approach that emphasizes the motives or "good faith" of the state agency involved: From democracy's standpoint, what matters is not what the agency is trying to do but what it has in fact done. To assess the validity of the state intervention the reviewing court must ask, directly and unequivocally, whether the intervention in fact enriches rather than impoverishes public debate.

This is no easy question, especially when we proceed, as we must, without Marcuse's guidance as to what kind of views are to be allowed in a democracy. We must be certain everything worth saying is said, but what is worth saying? In answering this question and in trying to construct the norms that are to ensure the robustness of debate, we may find help in the old notion that it is easier to identify an injustice than to explain what is justice. In the racial area,[34] we have proceeded in this negative fashion, trying to identify impermissible effects ("group disadvantaging," "disproportionate impact," etc.), without a commitment to a particular end-state. I suspect that is how we must proceed in the First Amendment domain as well. In fact, the notions of "drowning out" or "domination,"[35] used by Justice White on various occasions to explain how social or economic power under a regime of autonomy might distort public debate, strike me as gestures in this direction. They are, of course, only a beginning, and perhaps a small one at that, and we should have no illusion about how long and how difficult a journey lies ahead.

Realism is not, however, the same as pessimism, and in these matters I tend to be optimistic. I believe in reason and in the deliberate and incremental methods of the law: The courts are no more disabled from giving content to the enrichment of public debate idea than to any other (including autonomy). I am also sustained by my belief in the importance—no, the urgency—of the journey that the structuralist has invited us to take. Unless we stop the by now quite tiresome incantation of Brennan's formula, and begin to explain precisely what we mean when we speak of a debate that is "uninhibited, robust, and wide-open," and to assess various interventions and strategies in light of their contribution toward that end, we will never establish the effective precondition of a true democracy.

V

I do not expect everyone to share my optimism. I can understand someone who acknowledges how social structure and the protection of autonomy might skew public debate, but may conclude that the inquiries called for by the structuralist approach are too difficult or too dangerous. Such a position would be but an acknowledgment of the tragic condition in which we live—we know what freedom requires, but find it too difficult or too dangerous to act on its behalf. But that was not the posture of the controlling bloc of the Supreme Court in the free speech cases of the seventies. The Court did not, for example, present its decision to invalidate the Massachusetts law limiting corporate political expenditures as a tragedy, where, on the one hand, it acknowledged how the "domination" that Justice White described might interfere with First Amendment values but, on the other, explained that it might be too dangerous or too difficult even to entertain the possibility of corrective measures by the state. Rather, Justice Powell announced the Court's decision as a full and triumphant vindication of First Amendment values. It is this stance, above all, that I find most troubling, and that has led me to wonder whether the real source of the problem was not the Justices, but rather the tradition.

Some of the Justices recognized the divergence between autonomy and rich public debate, and seemed prepared to honor and further the public debate value at the expense of autonomy. Now and then they were prepared to work in patient and disciplined ways to make certain that the intervention challenged enriched rather than impoverished public debate. At their finest moments, they were attentive to questions of institutional design and the danger of First Amendment counterproductivity. Here I am thinking especially of Justices White and Brennan, though even they sometimes stumbled under the weight of the tradition. The method of the prevailing majority, perhaps best typified by the work of Justice Powell, was, however, of another character entirely. For them, it was all autonomy—as though we were back on the street corner and the function of the First Amendment was simply to stop the policeman. Their method *was* the tradition.

One part of their method was to see a threat to autonomy whenever the state acted in a regulatory manner: For example, Justice Powell feared that a law requiring access to a shopping center might have the effect of compromising the free speech rights of the owners[36]—the Fourteenth Amendment may not have enacted the *Social Statics* of Mr. Herbert Spencer, but maybe the First Amendment did. The autonomy of the owners will be compromised, Justice Powell argued, because there is a risk that views of the political activists will be attributed to them. Faced with the fact that the activists gained access by force of law and under conditions that provide access to all, and that, in any event, the owners could protect against the risk of attribution by posting signs disclaiming any support for the views espoused, Justice Powell moved his search for autonomy to an even more absurd level. He insisted that being forced to post a disclaimer might itself be a violation of the autonomy guaranteed by the First Amendment.[37] For some strange reason, Justice White joined this opinion.

Another part of the method of the prevailing majority was to treat autonomy as a near absolute and as the only First Amendment value. The enrichment of public debate would be an agreeable by-product of a regime of autonomy (they too quote the Brennan formula), but what the First Amendment commands is the protection of autonomy—individual or institutional—and if that protection does not enrich public debate, or somehow distorts it, so be it. To be sure, the fairness doctrine has been tolerated, but largely out of respect for precedent, or a deference to the legislative or administrative will, and was distinguished on rather fatuous grounds. The Court made clear that the FCC was free to abandon it, and in any event, the doctrine and the regulation of content that it implies were not to be extended to the print media. Curbs on financial contributions to candidates were permitted once again out of deference to precedent, and as a way of curbing corruption, but curbs on expenditures were invalidated as interfering with the autonomy supposedly guaranteed by the First Amendment. These are the decisions that gave the seventies its special character. Reflecting the full power of the received tradition, time and time again, the Court declared: "[T]he concept that government may restrict the speech of some elements of our society in order to enhance the relative voice of others is wholly foreign to the First Amendment. . . . "[38]

Autonomy is an idea that is especially geared to the state acting in a regulatory manner—it is the shield against the policeman. When the state acts affirmatively, say through the provisions of subsidies or benefits, the tradition does not have much to say. As a result, during this same period the Supreme Court was, much to my relief, more tolerant of such state intervention, but that tolerance was achieved at the price of coherence. The Court had no standard to guide its review. Rather than asking whether the action in question enriched debate, the Justices tried to reformulate the issue in terms of the received tradition. In a case involving the withdrawal from a school library of allegedly scandalous books like Eldridge Cleaver's *Soul on Ice*, Justice Brennan found himself obliged to cast this act of censorship—a transparent attempt to narrow debate—into an infringement of autonomy and a violation of the rule against content regulation.[39] This led him to make an untenable distinction between the removal and acquisition of books, and to look into the motives of the school board—a type of inquiry for which, as he demonstrated in other contexts, he had no taste whatsoever. Even then, he was unable to secure a majority.

In this case, and in others that involved the state in some capacity other than policeman, Justice Brennan and his allies faced a high-pitched dissent by Justice Rehnquist, in which he made explicit the distinction between when the state acts as sovereign (policeman) and when it acts in other capacities (e.g., as educator, employer, financier).[40] For the latter category, Justice Rehnquist argued for a standard that would leave the state with almost total discretion. In this regard he spoke for others, and in a later case[41] secured a majority and wrote the prevailing opinion (which Justice Brennan joined—a fact he later regretted).[42] It seems to me, however, that what the First Amendment requires in these cases is not indifference, but a commitment on the part of the Court to do all that it can possibly do to support and encourage the state in efforts to enrich public debate, to eliminate those restrictions of its subsidy programs that would narrow and restrict public debate, and if need be, even to require the state to continue and embark on programs that enrich debate.[43] The problem of remedies and the limits on institutional competence may, in the last instance, cause the Justices—even one so strong in his conception of office as Justice Brennan—to retreat from such an ambitious undertaking, but such a failure of nerve, or exercise in prudence, should be recognized for what it is: a compromise, not a vindication of the First Amendment or democratic values.

When subsidies were involved, the Court allowed the state to act—the Court was torn and the opinions were incoherent, but the First Amendment was not viewed as a bar to state action. When confronted with regulatory measures, however, such as ceilings and limits on political expenditures, the Court saw a threat to autonomy as defined by the tradition and reacted in a much more straightforward and much more restricted way: The state was stopped. In so reacting the Justices gave expression to the tradition, and our longstanding commitment to the tenets of classical liberalism and its plea for limited government. They also gave expression to the political mood of the day, which was—and still is, now more than ever—defined by its hostility to the activist state. Abolition of the fairness doctrine could be passed off as just one more instance of "deregulation." It seems to me, however, that there is much to regret in this stance of the Court and the tradition upon which it rested.

The received tradition presupposes a world that no longer exists and that is beyond our capacity to recall—a world in which the principal political forum was the street corner. The tradition ignores the manifold ways in which the state participates in the construction of all things social and how contemporary social structure will, if left to itself, skew public debate. It also makes the choices that we confront seem all too easy. The received tradition takes no account of the fact that to serve the ultimate purpose of the First Amendment we may sometimes find it necessary to "restrict the speech of some elements of our society in order to enhance the relative voice of others," and that unless the Court allows, and sometimes even requires, the state to do so, we as a people will never truly be free.

2
Why the State?

PROLOGUE

Nineteen eighty-seven marked the 100th anniversary of the Harvard Law Review, *and the editors invited a number of law teachers, including me, to write essays for an issue of the* Review *that was to celebrate this event.* Free Speech and Social Structure *had just been published, and I thought I would use the opportunity provided by the* Harvard Law Review *to refine the major argument of that essay. The presumption against the state that I had railed against seemed to be rooted in the theories of laissez-faire so rampant during the era in which the* Review *began. The context of my critique was narrow, in the sense that I dealt only with the First Amendment, but since that branch of constitutional law had long been the breeding ground of libertarian sentiment, it seemed to me that any victory achieved there would be an important one.*

While working on the essay, I became part of a study group sponsored by the Institute for Philosophy and Public Policy of the University of Maryland and chaired by Judith Lichtenberg. The focus of the group was on the mass media—which no doubt accounts for the emphasis in the essay that finally emerged on the fairness doctrine and other issues arising from state regulation of the press. In addition to constitutional lawyers, philosophers, and political theorists, the study group included a number of journalists and professors of journalism. Their presence made me consider more fully the possibility of professional self-regulation as an alternative to state regulation. The papers from the study group were edited by Professor Lichtenberg and published in 1990 under the title Democracy and the Mass Media. *The version of my paper that appears here was published in the February 1987 issue of the* Harvard Law Review.

W e're back where we began. One hundred years ago the issue of the day was the scope of state power. America was becoming increasingly urbanized and industrialized, and to curb the excesses of industrial capitalism, various political forces turned to the state.[1] The Interstate Commerce Commission was established in 1887, as part of a larger program to regulate the railroads that was to include the Elkins Act of 1903, the Hepburn Act of 1906, and many state statutes. Congress enacted the Sherman Act in 1890 and the first peacetime income tax in 1894. Statutes were also passed regulating the sale and distribution of liquor and lotteries, and a large number of measures were enacted at both the federal and state level to control various facets of the employment relationship, including the maximum number of hours worked, safety, child labor, and union membership.

These advances in the use of state power did not come easily. They were fought at almost every turn, and the forces of resistance found a sympathetic ear in the Supreme Court. Many of the measures were invalidated, while others were cabined by narrow constructions. Liberty was reduced to limited government. During the early part of the twentieth century, however, the balance of power began to shift, and by the time of the New Deal and World War II, state intervention in social and economic matters became a pervasive feature of national life. In the modern period, the victory of the activist state was given dramatic expression in the civil rights movement of the early 1960s—the so-called Second Reconstruction—and in Lyndon Johnson's Great Society. State power became the principal instrument for achieving a true and substantive equality.

In the late sixties, as our attention shifted to the Vietnam War and we began to feel the pressure of a spiraling inflation, things changed. An attack on "big government" became the organizing theme of our politics. It was voiced by both Democrats and Republicans, and over the next twenty years a myriad of programs were proposed and sometimes instituted to limit domestic governmental activities, particularly those of the federal government. These programs went by the name of "the new federalism," "revenue sharing," "deregulation," "privatization," "balancing the budget," and "alternative dispute resolution." Virtually all of the political leaders of the period partook in this assault on the activist state, but none more successfully than President Reagan. He pushed for the recriminalization of abortion, but putting that issue to one side, he managed to put the activist state on the defensive and to call into question the principles that had, for a generation or two, been taken as axiomatic. Today we find ourselves engaged in the same debates that dominated law and politics a century ago; only the burden of revision has changed. The issue is still the reach of state power, but the debate now takes place in a social context in which the activist state is part of the status quo.

In this debate, as in all the grand struggles of American politics, the Constitution has played an important role. Critics of the activist state invoke the Due Process Clause and its protection of liberty, but with only limited success. It has given rise to a "right to privacy" and has been used to protect the right to an abortion, but only by the narrowest of margins. *Lochner v. New York,*[2] the 1905 Supreme Court decision that invalidated a state statute establishing a ceiling on the number of hours worked each week, still operates as a negative example, as a reminder of all the dangers of substantive due process. There is, however, another branch of constitutional law that does not labor under this historical burden and that has long served as the breeding ground of libertarian sentiment. It is the First Amendment.

As a protection of speech and other forms of political activity, the First Amendment is more limited in its reach than substantive due process, which can be used as a bar to all manner of state regulation. But those intent on attacking state intervention have learned how to bring more and more activities within the protection of the First Amendment; today it is even used to curb state regulation of commercial advertising. The First Amendment also enjoys what substantive due process was never able to obtain, namely, a consensus—support from the entire political spectrum. Even as pressure mounted in the early part of this century for increased state intervention, a special place or exception was always reserved for speech. The progressives embraced Holmes's dissent in *Abrams v. United States,*[3] and its plea for "free trade in ideas,"[4] just as fervently as they did his dissent in *Lochner.* In fact, free speech achieved its first victories in the Supreme Court just when the Court began the process of overruling *Lochner* and legitimating the New Deal.

This peculiar status of free speech in our constitutional scheme, as the one plea for limited government that appears to be embraced by all, has not gone unnoticed by free market theorists. As part of the contemporary assault on state activism that so dominates our politics, Ronald Coase and Aaron Director have confronted New Deal liberals with the free speech tradition in order to remind them of the virtues of laissez-faire and to build a case against state intervention in economic matters.[5]

My inclination is, of course, just the reverse. It occurred to me that if Coase and Director can celebrate the libertarian element in the free speech tradition as a way of arguing against state intervention in the economic sphere, we should be able to start at the other end—to begin with the fact of state intervention in economic matters, and then use that historical experience to understand why the state might have a role to play in furthering free speech values. Such an approach might not only clarify and enrich our understanding of the First Amendment, but might also yield a more general and perhaps more important insight. It might undermine the larger assault on the state. Because speech has been used as a lever for laissez-faire, on the theory that speech is the area where the demand for limited government is strongest and most appealing, a conclusion that state regulation of speech is consistent with, and may even be required by, the First Amendment might well throw the entire critique of the activist state into question.

This essay focuses on the First Amendment and the role of the state in furthering free speech values, but is situated within a broader debate, as vibrant in 1987 as it was in 1887, about the role of the state in general, and it is meant to illuminate that larger issue as well. Far from what Coase and Director supposed, the First Amendment does not supply considerations in favor of laissez-faire, but rather points toward the necessity of the activist state.

I

The Constitution is not a testamentary document that distributes to future generations pieces of property in the form of rights. Rather, it is a charter of governance that establishes the institutions of government and the norms, standards, and principles that are to control those institutions. The Bill of Rights assumes that the institutions of government have already been established and proceeds to make authoritative a set of social ideals or values. Adjudication is one process by which these abstract ideals are given concrete meaning and expression and are thereby translated into rights.

In the case of the Equal Protection Clause, the taproot of modern law, this general picture of constitutional adjudication is now well established, although we have also come to recognize that constitutional ideals are susceptible to various interpretations. There appears to be agreement on the purpose of the Fourteenth Amendment; it was intended to secure equality for the newly freed slaves and to give constitutional status to the ideal of racial equality. There has been disagreement, however, over the particular principles or rules that should be applied to realize this ideal.

At first it seemed that a principle prohibiting discrimination and commanding color blindness would be appropriate. But during the Second Reconstruction, as we moved away from the problems of Jim Crow and began to confront more deeply entrenched forms of racism, we had second thoughts. A new principle seemed necessary, one that could directly and immediately protect against the perpetuation or aggravation of caste structure. I called this new principle "the group disadvantaging principle,"[6] but more recently it has come to be known as the "anticaste or antisubordination principle." The group disadvantaging principle seeks to promote racial equality, as does the antidiscrimination one, but understands racial equality in substantive rather than procedural terms. The group disadvantaging principle does not aim at guaranteeing color blindness, but rather seeks to end social subordination.

In the modern period, equal protection litigation can be seen as a struggle between these two mediating principles—between two conflicting visions of how the commitment to racial equality should be understood and how the ideal might be most effectively realized. In a number of cases the two principles have diverged, most notably when courts are asked to evaluate selection criteria (such as job tests) that appear neutral on their face but have an adverse impact on a disadvantaged group. Antidiscrimination permits such criteria, while the group disadvantaging principle tends to bar them. Furthermore, on some occasions, a conflict has arisen between the two principles, as when blacks have been given a preference in hiring in order to improve their social position. The group disadvantaging principle permits, and might even require, such treatment for blacks. The antidiscrimination principle, with its commitment to color blindness, tends to make such treatment illegal.

These struggles over the meaning of equal protection have given our constitutional age its special character, and after having been immersed in them for a decade or two, it is not at all surprising that I see within the First Amendment a similar intellectual process. Most agree that the underlying purpose of the First Amendment is to protect collective self-determination in much the same way that the underlying purpose of the Fourteenth Amendment is to protect racial equality, but we are once again divided over the mediating principle that gives fullest expression to that underlying purpose. Here the division is not between antidiscrimination and group disadvantaging, as it is in equal protection, but rather between autonomy and public debate. These two principles represent different ways of understanding and furthering the democratic purposes of the First Amendment. The distinction between the autonomy principle and the public debate principle is, moreover, crucial for explaining why the state has a role to play in furthering free speech values.

Those who reduce the First Amendment to a limit on state action tend to regard it as a protection of autonomy. The individual is allowed to say what he or she wishes, free from state interference. It is as though a zone of noninterference were placed around each individual, and the state (and only the state) were prohibited from crossing the boundary. Even in this account, however, autonomy is not protected as an end in itself, nor as a means of individual self-actualization. Rather, it is seen as a way of furthering the larger political purposes attributed to the First Amendment. It is assumed that the protection of autonomy will produce a debate on issues of public importance that is, to use Justice Brennan's formula, "uninhibited, robust, and wide-open."[7] Of course, rich public debate will not itself ensure self-governance, because the electorate must still listen to what is said and act on the basis of what it learns, but free and open debate still remains an essential precondition for democratic government, and autonomy is seen as the method of bringing that debate into being.

Some may dispute this instrumental view of autonomy, but it is embraced by people as far apart on the political spectrum as Harry Kalven and Robert Bork and now dominates our thinking about the First Amendment. It is rooted in the fact that the free speech guarantee appears as part of a legal instrument, the Constitution, which is for the most part concerned with establishing the structure of government. The instrumental theory also explains why speech, among the many ways of self-actualization, is singled out by the Constitution,[8] why the autonomy protected under the First Amendment could belong to institutions (CBS or the NAACP) as well as to individuals, and why speech could be preferred even when it harms someone else and thus infringes on that person's efforts at self-actualization.[9] The linkage between autonomy and democracy also accounts for the favored position in First Amendment jurisprudence of the rule against content regulation. The hope is that a rule denying the state the power to silence speech on the basis of its content will produce the broadest possible debate.

In some social settings, the instrumental assumption underlying the protection of autonomy may be well founded. In a Jeffersonian democracy, for example, where the dominant social unit is the individual and power is distributed equally, autonomy might well enhance public debate and thus promote collective self-determination. But in modern society, characterized by grossly unequal distributions of power and a limited capacity of people to learn all that they must to function effectively as citizens, this assumption is problematic. Protecting autonomy by placing a zone of non-interference around the individual, or certain institutions, is likely to produce a public debate that is dominated, and thus constrained, by the same forces that dominate our social structure, not a debate that is "uninhibited, robust, and wide-open."

The public debate principle, in contrast, acknowledges the problematic character of the instrumental assumption underlying the protection of autonomy and seeks to provide a foundation for the necessary corrective action. The purpose of the First Amendment remains what it was under autonomy—to protect the ability of the people, as a collectivity, to decide their own fate. Rich public debate also continues to appear as an essential precondition for the exercise of that sovereign prerogative. But now action is judged by its impact on public debate, viewed as a social state of affairs, rather than by whether it constrains or otherwise interferes with the autonomy of some individual or institution. The concern is not with the frustration of would-be speakers, but with the quality of public discourse. Autonomy may be protected, but only when it enriches public debate. It might well have to be sacrificed when, for example, the speech of some drowns out the voices of others or systematically distorts the public agenda.

Disfavoring state action is not the same as precluding such action altogether. Those who read the First Amendment as a protection of autonomy are not necessarily committed to the absolutist position identified with Justice Black (who insisted that "no law" means "no law").[10] They sometimes allow the state to cross the boundary and interfere with autonomy in order to serve other social interests; speakers may, for example, be silenced to preserve public order or to protect interests in reputation. What the autonomy principle does, however, is create a very strong presumption against state interference with speech. But under the public debate principle, there is no such presumption against the state. The state stands on equal footing with other institutions and is allowed, encouraged, and sometimes required to enact measures or issue decrees that enrich public debate, even if that action entails an interference with the speech of some and thus a denial of autonomy.

Of course, the state might act wrongfully, and thereby restrict or impoverish rather than enhance public debate. We must always stand on guard against this danger, but we should do so mindful of the fact that this same danger is presented by all social institutions, private or public, and that there is no reason for *presuming* that the state will be more likely to exercise its power to distort public debate than would any other institution. It has no special incentive to do so; government officials like to preserve their positions and the system that brought them to power, but the same can be said of the owners and managers of so-called private enterprises, who might well use their power to protect themselves and those government officials who serve their interests. Admittedly, the state does have some unique resources at its disposal, including a monopoly over the lawful means of violence, but once we cease to think of the state as a monolith (the Leviathan) and realize that it is a network of competing and overlapping agencies, one checking another and all being checked by private institutions, that power will appear less remarkable and less fearsome. We will come to see that the state's monopoly over the lawful infliction of violence is not a true measure of its power and that the power of an agency, like the FCC, is no greater than that of CBS. Terror comes in many forms. The powers of the FCC and CBS differ, one regulates while the other edits, but there is no reason to believe that one kind of power will be more limiting of public debate than the other. The state, like any other institution, can act either as a friend or an enemy of speech, and without falling back on the libertarian presumption, we must learn to recognize when it is acting in one capacity rather than another.

II

Today, public debate is dominated by the television networks and a number of large newspapers and magazines. The competition among these institutions is far from perfect, and some might argue for state intervention on a theory of market failure. There is a great deal of force to those arguments, but they obscure a deeper truth, namely, that a market, even one that is working perfectly, is itself a structure of constraint. A fully competitive market might produce a diversity of programs, formats, and reportage, but, to borrow an image of Renata Adler's, it will be the diversity of "a pack going essentially in one direction."[11]

The market constrains the presentation of matters of public interest and importance in two ways. First, the market privileges select groups by making programs, journals, and newspapers especially responsive to their needs and desires. One such group consists of those who have the capital to acquire or own a television station, newspaper, or journal; another consists of those who control the advertising budgets of various businesses; and still another consists of those who are most able and most likely to respond enthusiastically to advertising. The number in the last group is no doubt quite large (it probably includes every nine-year-old who can bully his or her parents into purchasing one thing or another), but it is not coextensive with the electorate. To be a consumer, even a sovereign one, is not to be a citizen.

Second, the market brings to bear on editorial and programming decisions factors that might have a great deal to do with profitability or allocative efficiency (to look at matters from a societal point of view), but little to do with the democratic needs of the electorate. For a business, the costs of production and the revenue likely to be generated are highly pertinent factors in determining what shows to run and when, or what to feature in a newspaper; a perfectly competitive market will produce shows or publications whose marginal cost equals marginal revenue. Reruns of *I Love Lucy* are profitable and an efficient use of resources. So is MTV. But there is no necessary, or even probabilistic, relationship between making a profit (or allocating resources efficiently) and supplying the electorate with the information it needs to make free and intelligent choices about government policy, the structure of government, or the nature of society. This point was well understood when we freed our educational systems and our universities from the grasp of the market, and it applies with equal force to the media.

None of this is meant to denigrate the market. It is only to recognize its limitations. The issue is not market failure but market reach. The market might be splendid for some purposes but not for others. It might be an effective institution for producing cheap and varied consumer goods and for providing essential services (including entertainment), but not for producing the kind of debate that constantly renews the capacity of a people for self-determination. The state is to act as the much-needed countervailing power, to counteract the skew of public debate attributable to the market and thus preserve the essential conditions of democracy. The purpose of the state is not to supplant the market (as it would under a socialist theory), nor to perfect the market (as it would under a theory of market failure), but rather to supplement it. The state is to act as the corrective *for* the market. The state must put on the agenda issues that are systematically ignored and slighted, and it must enable us to hear voices and viewpoints that would otherwise be silenced or muffled.

To turn to the state for these reasons does not presuppose that the people who staff a government agency are different in moral quality or in personality from those who control or manage the so-called private media. The state has no corner on virtue. What the theory of countervailing power does presuppose, however, is that simply by force of their position government employees are subject to a different set of constraints than those who run the media. They are public officials. We know that sometimes the word "public" becomes hollow and empty, a mere cover for the advancement of private interests, and that systems of public accountability are not perfect. But that is not to deny the force of these systems of accountability altogether. They may be imperfect but nonetheless of some effect. There is also an important difference of aspiration. It is one thing to empower someone called a public official and to worry whether the power entrusted is being used for public ends; it is another thing simply to leave that power in the hands of those who openly and unabashedly serve institutions that rest on private capital and are subject to market pressures.

In recent years there has been increasing talk among journalists about professionalism, and it has been suggested that a new professional ethos exists today that will temper the influence of the market on journalists, editors, and program managers and strengthen their democratic resolve. Such a development is, of course, salutary, but it does not render state intervention unnecessary. Indeed, the growth of professional norms emphasizing the democratic rather than economic mission of the media might be traced in part to various state interventions, such as the fairness doctrine, which requires that broadcasters cover issues of public importance and do so fairly. Moreover, whatever the cause, the fact remains that these norms must be continuously reinforced by state intervention or other forms of institutionalized power if they are to be capable of resisting the pressures of the marketplace. As we know from *Brown v. Board of Education*[12] and the civil rights movement of the sixties, exemplary "folkways" can sometimes be nourished, and maybe even created or legitimated, by strong exercises of state power.

Drawing on the power of taxation and its organizational advantages, the state can discharge its corrective function through the provision of subsidies. Examples of this form of state intervention include aid to public libraries, public schools, private and state universities, public broadcasting, and presidential candidates. These subsidies make an enormous contribution to public discourse and further First Amendment values, although we would never know it from a reading of the First Amendment that emphasizes the protection of autonomy. Autonomy is not a bar to such state activities, but it does produce a constitutional indifference, leaving these activities to suffer the vicissitudes of a politics itself dominated by the market. Under the public debate principle such action is favored, and when inaction becomes a form of action, it may also be required, although the remedial problems of implementing such an affirmative duty are acute and well known.[13]

With respect to the other form of state intervention—state action of a regulatory or prohibitory nature—the autonomy principle does have strong legal implications, and some of those are most unfortunate. The strong presumption against the state rooted in the autonomy principle has, for example, resulted in the invalidation of laws imposing ceilings on campaign expenditures. It has also placed a constitutional cloud over the fairness doctrine, precluding the extension of that doctrine to the print media, enfeebling its enforcement, and putting its very existence in question. Autonomy provides the proponents of deregulation with a constitutional platform that is ill-deserved.

III

For most of the last twenty or thirty years the Right has dominated American politics, and it is the Right that has commandeered the assault on the activist state. By "the Right" I mean those who are prepared to accept as just or even natural the distribution of wealth and power produced by the market, and who seek to curb the state because of its reconstructive capacity and propensity. There are others, however, who are critical of the present distribution of wealth and power, but who are also wary of the state, particularly the one headquartered in Washington. They, too, have denounced the activist state and in its place urge not a return to the market, but a program of "Left decentralization."

A century ago, such a program was advanced by the populists, at least until they became absorbed into the mainstream and buckled under the organizational imperatives of the Democratic Party.[14] In the 1960s, the program of Left decentralization played an important role in the life of SNCC and SDS. Today, it is put forward by a group of academics located in (of all places) the law schools: the critical legal studies movement. Their critique of the activist state is not backed by even a modicum of political power (to put the point most generously), but I nonetheless feel compelled to respond, because it has captured the imagination of many people I respect and admire, above all my students, and because it builds on the premises that justify state intervention in the first place—a rejection of autonomy, an acceptance of the public debate principle, and an acknowledgment of the distorting influence of the market on democratic politics.

We began, you will recall, with the claim that, left to itself, public debate will not be "uninhibited, robust, and wide-open," but instead will be skewed by the forces that dominate society. The state should be allowed to intervene, and sometimes even required to do so, I argued, to correct for the market. In saying this, I assumed that the state would act as a countervailing power, but there is a danger, so the advocate of decentralization insists, that the state will not act in this way but will instead become the victim of the same forces that dominate public debate. There is a risk that the state will reinforce rather than counteract the skew of the market, because the state is as much an object of social forces as it is an agent of change. The state might do some good, but the prospect of this is so slim, and the danger of the opposite so great, that it would be best, the Left-leaning critic concludes, to bar state intervention altogether or at least to create a strong presumption against it—not to secure autonomy, but to ensure the richness of public debate.

In the late 1970s, Charles Lindblom published an important book, *Politics and Markets,* which described with great force and clarity the so-called danger of "circularity."[15] The state was supposed to govern business, but there was good reason to believe that the system of control largely worked the other way around. The picture that Lindblom painted was a sobering one—the danger of circularity is indeed real. But my own view of the facts and, more particularly, of our historical experience with the activist state in the sixties leads me to believe that the elements of independence possessed by the state are real and substantial. This independence is not complete, but it is nonetheless sufficient to make the theory of countervailing power viable. I also believe that we might cope with the danger of circularity in ways other than creating the strong presumption against state action urged by the proponents of decentralization. To begin with, we might recognize that some state agencies are more independent of market forces than others and accordingly we might allocate more power to them.

In the past, First Amendment jurisprudence has allowed the courts to play an important role in evaluating the intervention of various political agencies, in order to avoid the tyranny of the majority. I believe we should continue that tradition, but now as a way of gaining some measure of protection against circularity. The courts are part of the state and obviously are not wholly independent of the forces that dominate social structure, but they are likely to achieve a greater measure of independence than the legislature or administrative agencies. As we saw in the early New Deal, sometimes the courts achieve too much independence from social forces. This independence stems from the fact that judges have long, and sometimes even life, tenure; they are subject to well-established professional norms that require them to respond to grievances they might prefer to ignore; and they must justify their decisions publicly on the basis of principle.

The danger of circularity also might be reduced by changes in the design of particular institutions. The aim is not to free the various agencies of the state from the forces that dominate social structure (surely an impossible task), but only to make it more likely that these agencies will exert a countervailing force. This goal might be achieved by creating within these agencies certain processes or mechanisms that would enhance the power of the weaker elements in society (for example, creating offices of public advocacy in administrative agencies) and that would lessen the power of those who already dominate social structure (for example, establishing open-hearing requirements). In this way, the program advanced by Ralph Nader and other consumer advocates might have a First Amendment basis, because in fighting "agency capture" we might be increasing the independence of the state from the market and thus enhancing its capacity to correct for the constraints that social structure imposes on public debate. Such reform measures need not, of course, be confined to administrative agencies; they can extend to all agencies of the state, including the courts.

None of these ameliorative measures will eliminate the danger of circularity altogether. We should recognize their incompleteness and be cautious. But to do more, as the Left-leaning advocate of decentralization insists, and to join in the attack on the activist state that is so fashionable today, would expose us to an even greater danger: politics dominated by the market. We would be left without a remedy. Circularity is typically raised as an objection to regulatory action by the state when, for example, a prohibition backed by criminal sanctions is enforced against an individual or some institutional speaker. It is hard to understand, however, why the same objection does not also extend to the subsidy programs of the state. Some may favor those programs over regulatory measures on the theory that they do not violate autonomy, but since rich public debate rather than autonomy is for me, and the critic from the Left, the key First Amendment value, it would be hard for us to transform that preference into a constitutional rule. Under the public debate principle, the fairness doctrine and public television stand on the same constitutional plane: If one fails because of circularity, so must the other.

Overwhelmed by the fear of circularity, many on the Left would do away with all forms of state intervention. But they are not without hope—they project their ideals onto other institutions. They might turn their backs on the regulatory measures of the activist state and even denounce state subsidies, determined as they are to free democracy from the grasp of market forces, but they celebrate self-organization and modes of expression within the reach of every citizen like picketing and parading. Such activities, of course, have an important role to play in any account of the First Amendment and indeed are essential for a true and effective democracy. The civil rights marches of the sixties, the protests against the Vietnam War, the shanties raised on our campuses in protest of apartheid, and the historic movement in Poland known as Solidarity bear ample and glorious witness to this fact. The issue is not, however, whether self-organization and demonstration are necessary, but whether they are sufficient, at least to the point of justifying the attack on the activist state. This they surely are not. These activities are an important part of any First Amendment theory, but not adequate substitutes for the fairness doctrine, public television, restrictions on campaign expenditures, or other forms of state regulation or state subsidization aimed at enhancing the quality of public discourse.

In assessing the affirmative program of the Left, one should begin with the simple observation that the expressive activities that it favors do not eliminate the problem of circularity altogether. The state is often needed to legitimate and protect those activities, and there is no reason to be more suspicious of the state when it, for example, grants subsidies or regulates the media than when it regulates access to the shopping centers, silences hecklers, or legitimates and protects union activity.[16] Moreover, to rely exclusively, or even primarily, on parading or picketing (referred to by one of my colleagues, not a radical, as "cheap speech") would be to remit the least powerful elements in society to the least effective modes of expression. Compare one day's work of distributing pamphlets at a local shopping cen-

ter with a thirty-second editorial advertisement of the kind sought in
Columbia Broadcasting System v. Democratic National Committee.[17] Effective speech in the modern age is not cheap.

Things needn't be so. I can imagine a social setting in which the expressive activities celebrated by the Left would be sufficient. They might
work in the polis of ancient Greece or in an America divided, as Jefferson
proposed, into a multitude of little wards.[18] Then we would have a social
as opposed to a merely legal decentralization and a setting in which parading or picketing could effectively inform and educate the public as well as
develop the talents and shape the character of those individuals who participate in these activities. The attack on the activist state and the emphasis on cheap speech would not then be based just on a fear, the danger of
circularity, but could also make plausible claim to a theory of participa-
tory democracy. Such a theory would give the First Amendment program
of the Left its greatest appeal but, alas, it rests on an impossible dream. It
entails a division and reorganization of American society that is unlikely
ever to materialize. It presupposes a localism that is barely imaginable.

The Left-leaning proponents of decentralization are wary of the activist
state, and may have good reasons for that wariness, but in resurrecting the
presumption against the state, they offer no plausible alternative to a politics dominated by the market. They emphasize self-organization and direct
action such as parading and picketing, in contrast to state regulation or
state subsidization, but under the forms of social life we know, or are ever
likely to know, the forms of expression they celebrate would be insufficient. Something would be missing. The citizen would not be a consumer,
true, but I am afraid that he or she would be little more than an athlete (or
to use Arendt's metaphor, a flute player).[19] Politics would become a species
of performance. Those who happened to be engaged in the demonstration
would be ennobled and would feel the special pleasures of struggle and
contest, but for the most part the public—the voters—would sit by, unen-
gaged and unmoved by the spectacle, anxious to get on with the business
of the day.

In another world things might be different, but in this one we need the
state. In eschewing the tired and familiar presumption against the state, we
risk circularity, and a number of other dangers, but we do so to save our
democracy. We turn to the state because it is the most public of all our institutions and because only it has the power we need to resist the pressures
of the market and thus to enlarge and invigorate our politics.

3

Silence on the Street Corner

PROLOGUE

Justice Brennan spent the last two decades of his career on the Supreme Court in dissent. Now and then, he was able to salvage some of the Warren Court legacy, but most often, he found himself complaining of the retrenchment on rights by the majority. See A Life Lived Twice, *100* Yale Law Journal *1117 (1991). Free speech is sometimes portrayed as an area in which there is a consensus, but in truth these same divisions occurred in that domain as well. Although the controlling majority would often cite Justice Brennan's 1964 decision* in New York Times v. Sullivan, *it soon became clear that they had no taste for the value underlying that decision—robust public debate.*

Justice Brennan retired from the Court in June 1990. One of his very last opinions was a dissent in United States v. Kokinda, *in which the majority upheld a decision of the federal government denying political activists access to a public sidewalk. In his passionate and moving dissent, the Justice complained of the change in judicial doctrine that had occurred over the years and compared the prevailing position to that of the early 1960s, when the Court had heroically extended its arm to protect the civil rights demonstrations of the period. The Justice's dissent caught my eye and led me to use a number of the lectures to which I was already committed (at Albany Law School, Suffolk University Law School, and Princeton University) to explore the sad turn in the Court's doctrine. To establish a baseline, I reached back to the 1930s, described by Harry Kalven as the period when "speech started to win" (see* A Worthy Tradition, *page 167), and recovered one of the famed decisions of that era,* Schneider v. State. *The lecture was published in the Spring 1992* Suffolk University Law Review, *and soon thereafter in* Public Values in Constitutional Law *(Stephen Gottlieb, ed., 1993).*

A legal regime that does no more than protect the street corner speaker will not ensure a vibrant democracy. Today, the character of public debate is primarily determined not by what the street corner speaker has to say, nor by his or her capacity to engage the casual passerby, but rather by the media, especially television. Indeed, street corner activities, whether they be speeches, demonstrations, or parades, are staged largely for the television camera and obtain their power from appearing on the evening news.

Over the last two decades it has become increasingly difficult for radical critics of the status quo to obtain access to the mass media. In the late 1960s, the Supreme Court upheld a Federal Communications Commission (FCC) regulation—the fairness doctrine—which was aimed at broadening the spectrum of viewpoints heard on radio and television.[1] In the early 1970s, however, the Court reversed course. It held, first, that it would be unconstitutional for the state to grant access similarly to the print media[2] and, second, that even with respect to broadcasting, there was no obligation, statutory or constitutional, for the FCC to provide access for the direct expression of an editorial opinion.[3] Regulations such as the fairness doctrine were deemed purely optional. In the 1980s, this process continued along the same trajectory, and in 1987 the Reagan FCC renounced the fairness doctrine altogether.[4] Soon thereafter, the Court of Appeals for the District of Columbia upheld the FCC's decision as a permissible exercise of administrative discretion.[5]

The FCC remains under a statutory obligation, upheld by the Court, to police the networks to make certain that they provide adequate opportunity for presidential candidates to carry their message to the public.[6] But this arrangement provides little relief for more radical critics of the established order, since they tend to work outside the mainstream political culture and party organization. Similarly, the FCC policy giving preference to women and minorities in awarding or allocating licenses, also upheld by the Court,[7] is not likely to improve the situation markedly.

For one thing, those awarded licenses operate under market constraints; thus it is not entirely clear what difference the attempt to diversify ownership in terms of gender or race will make in the character of broadcasting. Moreover, the FCC does not seem especially committed to this ownership-diversification policy and is likely to implement it in a lax and

haphazard way. In fact, the FCC would have formally and openly abandoned the policy if Congress had not intervened. Finally, account must be
taken of the fact that the Supreme Court decision upholding the ownership-diversification policy was based on the narrowest of margins, five-to-
four, and a number of the majority, including Justices Brennan, Marshall,
and Blackmun, have since retired. The Court of Appeals for the District of
Columbia subsequently handed down an opinion—authored by Clarence
Thomas, Marshall's replacement—that cut back on that decision, holding
unconstitutional the aspect of the FCC policy which gives a preference to
women.[8]

The collapse of the legal regime that sought to broaden the expression
of differing views in the media does not close the door to radical critics
altogether. Some, especially the religious-based organizations, are
wealthy enough to buy air time, or even their own stations or newspapers.
Other dissident voices can be heard through "op-ed" essays, letters to the
editors, magazines of opinion, and broadcasts on public access cable
channels (for those who like to stay up in the wee hours of the night). The
events and activities of dissident groups are also covered by the networks
and major newspapers.

One does not want to ignore these speech opportunities altogether, but,
in truth, they are rather limited. Most radicals do not have the funds to buy
air time, the networks are reluctant to sell time to them anyway,
spokespersons for the underprivileged do not have the capital to buy a
newspaper or television station, and coverage of protest activities is cir-
cumscribed by the economic imperatives that drive the privately owned
media and today enfeeble public broadcasting.

In this context, we return to the street corner with a sense of despair. Its
significance for public debate pales compared to that of the mass media,
but it endures as one of the few arenas in which radical activists can make
an appeal to the public: The street corner is their last, desperate forum.
One would have hoped that the Supreme Court would accommodate the
changes it has wrought in the law governing the media by increasing the
protection of the street corner and other spaces that now are important locations of public social interaction, including bus terminals, airports, post
offices, and shopping malls. In fact, just the opposite has happened.
Rather than compensating for its media decisions by expanding the protection of alternative means of speech, the Court has pursued a policy
which aggravates or compounds the effect of those decisions. In doing so,
it has implied that the media decisions were not driven by a sensitivity to

the special needs of a free press, which are of course considerable, but rather by a lack of taste for, or perhaps even an aversion to, robust public debate.

I

Starting in 1939, in the famous case of *Schneider v. State,*[9] the street corner has been guarded by what I will call "the weighted balancing test." That test avoids definitional squabbles as to whether certain conduct— pamphleteering or picketing, for example—is "speech" rather than "action" by conceding to the state the power to pursue its interests in a way that has the added effect of restricting speech. The First Amendment operates not as an impenetrable shield around the speaker, creating an immunity against regulations that have the effect of limiting speech, but rather as a mechanism that structures the justificatory process. The street corner speaker can be silenced if, but only if, the state can demonstrate that it has an interest other than suppressing the expression of speech and that the significance of this interest outweighs the harm it causes to free speech.

The Court's opinion in *Schneider* was written by Justice Roberts. In a straightforward manner, refreshingly free of the jargon later used to characterize modern free speech decisions, he defined the task before him in these terms:

> In every case . . . where legislative abridgement of [First Amendment] rights is asserted, the courts should be astute to examine the effect of the challenged legislation. Mere legislative preferences or beliefs respecting matters of public convenience may well support regulation directed at other personal activities, but be insufficient to justify such as diminishes the exercise of rights so vital to the maintenance of democratic institutions. And so, as cases arise, the delicate and difficult task falls upon the courts to weigh the circumstances and to appraise the substantiality of the reasons advanced in support of the regulation of the free enjoyment of the rights.[10]

Schneider actually consisted of four different cases. One, of no special concern to us, involved an ordinance requiring a license for door-to-door canvassing. A Jehovah's Witness challenged that ordinance, and the Court struck it down under the authority of *Lovell v. Griffin*[11] as vesting the municipal authorities with too much discretion. The other three cases, unified by the fact that they involved local ordinances that prohibited distributing handbills or leaflets on the streets, are of great importance in illuminating what I have called the weighted balancing test.

In the first case, arising from Los Angeles, a person was convicted for distributing a handbill that advertised a meeting sponsored by the "Friends Lincoln Brigade," at which developments in the Spanish Civil War were to be discussed. The second case, coming from Milwaukee, involved a labor dispute at a meat market. One of the persons picketing the market was convicted for distributing handbills that set forth the position of the workers and asked persons to refrain from patronizing the market. The third case involved an ordinance against handbilling enacted by Worcester, Massachusetts; the handbills at issue announced a meeting to protest the way a state unemployment insurance program was being administered. In both this case and the one from Milwaukee there was ample evidence of the obvious—that many of the passersby who had received the handbills had discarded them, thereby littering the streets.

Except for a laconic dissent by Justice McReynolds, the Court was unanimous in setting aside the convictions for handbilling. The whole of Justice Roberts's analysis consisted of the following paragraph:

> The motive of the legislation under attack in [these handbilling cases] is held by the courts below to be the prevention of littering of the streets and, although the alleged offenders were not charged with themselves scattering paper in the streets, their convictions were sustained upon the theory that distribution by them encouraged or resulted in such littering. We are of opinion that the purpose to keep the streets clean and of good appearance is insufficient to justify an ordinance which prohibits a person rightfully on a public street from handing literature to one willing to receive it. Any burden imposed upon the city authorities in cleaning and caring for the streets as an indirect consequence of such distribution results from the constitutional protection of the freedom of speech and press. This constitutional protection does not deprive a city of all power to prevent street littering. There are obvious methods of preventing littering. Amongst these is the punishment of those who actually throw papers on the streets.[12]

In this passage, we can see the weighted balancing process at work. Roberts acknowledged the legitimacy of the state's interest in avoiding litter. Litter is aesthetically unpleasant, may be a health hazard, and requires additional expense on the part of government to clean up. However, these interests pale compared to the interest in free speech, which Roberts characterized earlier in the opinion as lying "at the foundation of free government by free men."[13] For Roberts, the scales were tipped in favor of free speech; as a result, the interests of the state must be especially worthy and important to save a statute restricting speech.

Even after deciding that the interest in avoiding litter is not sufficient to justify the interference with speech, Roberts pointed out, perhaps as a gesture of respect to the state, that the state has other alternatives for satisfying its interests. For example, the state could prosecute the passersby who actually threw the handbills in the street or on the sidewalk. Obviously, this strategy would be less effective and less efficient than going after the distributor of the handbills, but those sacrifices are considered the price for safeguarding the foundational freedom. As Harry Kalven phrased it years later, Roberts understood that free speech is not a luxury civil liberty.[14]

II

The full flowering of *Schneider* came in the 1960s, when the Warren Court used the weighted balancing test to protect the always passionate and sometimes disruptive speech activities of the civil rights movement.[15] Moved by the Court's heroic determination to keep the streets and sidewalks of the nation open to political activists, Harry Kalven added the concept of the "public forum" to the First Amendment lexicon and explained how access to that forum was central to a vibrant democracy.[16] In the 1970s and 1980s, however, the tide shifted, and the Court's protection of the street corner—née "public forum"—became increasingly less generous. *Schneider* remained on the books; it was frequently cited and discussed by the Court, but it was drained of all vitality.

One striking illustration of this development, and of the method by which Roberts's weighted balancing process has been transformed and distorted, is the Supreme Court's 1984 decision in *Los Angeles v. Taxpayers for Vincent*.[17] The case arose from a contest for the Los Angeles City Council and the effort of one of the candidates—Roland Vincent—to reach the public by posting signs on utility poles. The signs in question contained a simple message: "Roland Vincent—City Council." Acting under the authority of an ordinance that banned posting any signs on utility poles (or similar fixtures), city maintenance crews removed the signs. In response, Roland's supporters brought an injunctive suit in federal court attacking the ordinance as applied. By a divided vote, the Supreme Court, in an opinion by Justice Stevens, upheld the ordinance on the ground that it furthered various aesthetic interests, including the desire to avoid "visual clutter." Justices Brennan, Marshall, and Blackmun dissented.

The result in *Vincent* stands in bold contrast to that in *Schneider*, as does the method of analysis, though that is less obvious. In place of the weighted balancing test of *Schneider*, Stevens, building on a number of intervening precedents,[18] used a multitiered categorization approach. Under *Schneider*'s weighted balancing test, the governing metaphor is a scale especially rigged by the First Amendment: A thumb is placed on the side of speech, thereby requiring the state to produce, on the other side, an especially weighty or urgent interest in order for the regulation to survive. Under the categorization approach used in *Vincent*, the judge still considers two factors—the harm to speech and the state's interest. However, rather than balancing these factors, one against the other, the judge analyzes them in terms of two columns of pigeonholes or boxes. One column is for the harm, the other for the state's interest.

The first column classifies regulations according to the way they impinge on speech. A law that discriminates among speakers on the basis of content is to be classified as a "content regulation," whereas a law that regulates the time, place, or manner of speech belongs in a box that I will label "access regulation." The second column consists of three boxes for classifying the interest of the state furthered by the law. The first box is "compelling"; the second, "substantial"; and the third, "ordinary." Each indicates a different degree of importance for the state's interest.

The categorization approach also involves a set of rules, sometimes referred to as "tiers of scrutiny," that requires certain matches or linkages between the two columns, that is, between the type of speech-harm and the state interest. To be acceptable, a content regulation requires a state interest that falls in the "compelling" box; in other words, it is subject to the strictest or most exacting scrutiny. An access regulation is subject to a lesser or intermediate degree of scrutiny, because the state's interest need only be "substantial" or "significant."

In and of itself, the shift in metaphors, from a weighted balancing to a categorization approach, may be of no moment. It may simply be reflective of the ever-increasing bureaucratization of constitutional law, a way of administering a complex body of doctrine, posing no special danger to First

Amendment values.[19] As with the weighted balancing test, the categorization approach could respect the preferred status of free speech by always requiring that the state interest be "compelling." In that instance, there would be little difference between the two methods. Justice Roberts did not use the term "compelling," but he might as well have, because he required that the state interest be especially urgent in order to justify an abridgement of speech. A critical difference arises, however, because the movement to a categorization approach was accompanied by a lessening of the state's burden. "Compelling" is not the standard against which an access regulation like the Los Angeles ordinance is to be measured. Rather, such ordinances are to be judged under an intermediate standard—the interest served must be "substantial"—which is obviously more than "ordinary," but also less than "compelling."

In upholding the ordinance, the trial court in *Vincent* said the interest of Los Angeles in avoiding visual clutter was "legitimate and compelling."[20] This conclusion seems absurd on its face—if the desire to avoid visual clutter is a compelling interest, then the word compelling has been stripped of all its meaning. Justice Stevens ruled, however, that the city's interest need only be "significant" or "substantial."[21] The earlier cases teach, according to Stevens, that "the state may sometimes curtail speech when necessary to advance a significant and legitimate state interest."[22] He described the interest municipalities have in regulations of this type as "weighty,"[23] and concluded that "[t]he problem addressed by this ordinance—the visual assault on the citizens of Los Angeles presented by an accumulation of signs posted on public property—constitutes a significant substantive evil within the City's power to prohibit."[24]

Stevens's move to the intermediate standard of review was predicated on the view that the Los Angeles regulation was content neutral. The regulation did not by its terms single out Roland Vincent or political candidates in general, but rather applied to all persons wanting to use the utility poles. In taking this position, Stevens was faithful to a line of cases from the 1970s and early 1980s that singled out content regulation as especially threatening to First Amendment values. Precedent aside, however, a question can be raised about the soundness of his position. Barring one speaker or one category of speakers from the street corner is offensive, but so is a ban that shuts down the street corner altogether. It in effect disfavors those speakers who most need the street corner to reach the public and, in any event, reduces the overall quantity of public discussion, thereby impairing the public's capacity for self-determination. It was these concerns that moved the Court in *Schneider*, which, after all, in-

volved bans on handbilling that were, like the Los Angeles ban on posting signs, not content-specific.

Justice Stevens's willingness to lower the standard of review is a disturbing departure from *Schneider* and the public forum cases of the civil
rights era, but perhaps even more disturbing is how he applied the substantial interest test. At the very end of his opinion, he quoted the talismanic formula of *New York Times Co. v. Sullivan,* which spoke of the country's commitment to public debate that is "uninhibited, robust, and
wide-open."[25] Nowhere in his analysis, however, does the reader feel the
pull of this commitment. Stevens said that the interest in avoiding visual
clutter is "substantial" or "significant" or "weighty," but he used these
terms in a mechanical way, as though he were simply going through the
motions. Indeed, if the interest in avoiding visual clutter is sufficient to justify a ban on speech, there are few state interests that would not be.
Certainly, any of the reasons typically given to silence the street corner
speaker—to avoid traffic hazards, lessen pedestrian congestion, ensure
unimpeded access to stores, prevent breaches of the peace—would suffice.
Even the desire to avoid litter, based as it is on both health and aesthetic
considerations, would be sufficient to justify a ban on handbilling.
Nothing, absolutely nothing, would be left to *Schneider* and its progeny.

Faced with this disturbing result, Stevens pursued two lines of argument
which may be read as efforts to temper his position. The first suggests that
the state in *Vincent* had no alternative—it could not further its interests in
a way that would be significantly less threatening to First Amendment values. In the context of the weighted balancing process, this concern with alternative regulatory strategies is an integral part of the judgment about
whether the state's interest justifies the law in question. For example, in
Schneider the presence of a less restrictive alternative (specifically, the
statute making it a crime to litter) negated or undercut the claim that the
ban on handbills was compelled by an interest in avoiding litter. In the categorical approach of the modern cases, however, the inquiry into "less restrictive alternatives" appears as an additional requirement. The state interest must be substantial (or in some instances, compelling) *and* the
regulation must also be the least restrictive way of satisfying this interest.[26]
This means that in order to uphold the Los Angeles ordinance, Stevens had
to conclude not only that the avoidance of visual clutter was a substantial
interest, but also that the ordinance Los Angeles adopted was the least restrictive way of furthering that objective.

Clearly, there were less restrictive alternatives available in *Vincent*. As
Justice Brennan pointed out in dissent, instead of banning all posted signs

throughout Los Angeles, as the ordinance did, the city could have banned the posting of signs in some areas or it could have enacted measures to reduce the density of signs. Compared to a total ban, such measures may not have satisfied the city's aesthetic interest as fully or efficiently. But as *Schneider* indicated, the least-restrictive-alternative test requires that some sacrifices be made for the sake of free speech.

Justice Stevens avoided this conclusion, in part, by watering down the least-restrictive-alternative requirement of the modern cases. A regulation that impinges on speech will fall only if it is "substantially broader than necessary" to protect the state interest.[27] In other words, a regulation that is not the least restrictive alternative will be allowed to stand if it is not "substantially" more restrictive than other strategies available to the state. The burden on the state to seek out the *least* restrictive alternative is thereby reduced. Density regulations of the type Brennan proposed may be less restrictive than a total ban, but, according to Stevens, the state will not be restricted to them since they are not "substantially" less restrictive than the method of regulation chosen. Not every saving of speech is required, only substantial ones.

A similar disregard for the special importance of First Amendment values was manifested when, in the context of the least-restrictive-alternative inquiry, Stevens went on to distinguish *Schneider* itself, on the ground that the antilittering statute imagined by Justice Roberts would not have entailed an interference with speech, while the alternatives imagined by Brennan would have. Stevens wrote: "[A]n antilittering statute could have addressed the substantive evil without prohibiting expressive activity. . . . Here, the substantive evil—visual blight—is not merely a possible by-product of the activity, but is created by the medium of expression itself."[28]

In this passage, Stevens is accurately describing a difference between the two cases, but his effort to turn that difference into a limitation on the relevance of *Schneider* is unpersuasive. Roberts's mention in *Schneider* of the antilittering statute was intended as an example, to indicate that there are less restrictive alternatives to the ban on handbilling involved in that case.[29] What should control is not the example, but the rule, which requires the Court to ask whether there were less restrictive alternatives than the one chosen by Los Angeles, as there indeed were. Even if Brennan's alternatives would have entailed some interference with speech, that interference would have been less than that produced by the total ban in force in Los Angeles.

A second strategy for softening or excusing the result in *Vincent* may be found in Stevens's claim that the speaker had adequate alternative chan-

nels of communication. Specifically, Stevens wrote, "nothing in the find-
ings indicates that the posting of political posters on public property is a
uniquely valuable or important mode of communication, or that appellees'
ability to communicate effectively is threatened by ever-increasing restrictions on expression."[30] Trying to put an affirmative gloss on this statement, one might read Stevens as suggesting that, when there are no alternative channels, the state interest must be compelling (even though the
regulation in question is a general one), or that the state interest must be
truly substantial, or that the Court would apply the least-restrictive-alternative test more rigorously. Under this interpretation, when there are no
alternative channels, the loss to free speech is more egregious and there
will be more reason for the Court to be scrupulous in its review of the
state's action.

I find, however, little consolation in this part of Justice Stevens's analysis in *Vincent.* Rather than asking whether posting signs on utility poles is
a sensible and effective method of communicating with the public—
which is all one could ask about handbilling—Stevens seems to place the
burden on the speaker to demonstrate that the means of communication is
"uniquely valuable." Handbilling, or any other mode of communication,
when taken by itself, cannot possibly meet this test. There are always alternatives, some better than others, but no single mode of communication
is "uniquely valuable."

Justice Roberts in *Schneider* approached the question of alternative av-
enues of communication from a different perspective. He respected the
choice of the speaker concerning the means by which he or she would try
to reach the public and then placed the burden on the state to justify interferences with that choice. As he put it, "[O]ne is not to have the exercise of his liberty of expression abridged on the plea that it may be exercised in some other place."[31] In contrast, Justice Stevens seems prepared
to put the burden of justification on the state only after the speaker has justified his or her choice of the means of communication, and has done so
in some compelling way.

III

While the Court in *Vincent* subtly manipulated the weighted balancing test
and its modern counterpart to produce a result fundamentally at odds with
Schneider, it nominally adhered to a watered-down version of the test. The

Court promised an intermediate measure of scrutiny, though, as we saw, that promise was thoroughly breached in the application. However, in *United States v. Kokinda,*[32] a 1990 decision, the revisionary process took a further turn, virtually repudiating *Schneider* and all that it represents. In an opinion by Justice O'Connor, a plurality of the Justices openly abandoned any special review, by either weighted balancing or intermediate scrutiny, of a large class of regulations that restrict access to public property, including sidewalks. Justice Kennedy refused to join O'Connor's opinion. He insisted that some intermediate measure of scrutiny be applied, although, in the spirit of *Vincent,* upon which he relied, he found that test satisfied. Justices Brennan, Marshall, and Blackmun dissented once again. This time they were joined by Justice Stevens.

At issue in *Kokinda* was a regulation of the United States Postal Service prohibiting the solicitation of funds on its property. The regulation was applied to a group of volunteers for a political organization who had set up a table on the sidewalk near the entrance of a post office to solicit contributions, to take orders for books and subscriptions to the organization's newspaper, and to distribute literature addressing a variety of political issues.

The post office in question was a free-standing building on a major highway in suburban Maryland. People drove to the post office, parked in the parking lot, and then walked from their cars to the post office on the sidewalk used by the political activists for their solicitations. The solicitors were subjected to criminal prosecution and appeared very much like the picketers in front of the Milwaukee meat market in *Schneider.* There was, however, one crucial difference: The sidewalk was owned and constructed by the United States Postal Service rather than the city.

The government defended its action on the ground that solicitations impeded the normal flow of traffic in and out of the post office, thereby interfering with the much-heralded program of the Postal Service to become more efficient. There were three responses to this argument. The dissenters, who spoke through Justice Brennan, in one of his very last opinions, acknowledged the legitimacy of the government's interest in efficiency, but thought it was insufficient to justify the interference with speech. The dissenters were faithful to *Schneider.* A second response was set forth in Justice Kennedy's concurring opinion. He was prepared to uphold the prosecution on the theory that the interest of facilitating traffic flow qualified as a "substantial," "significant," or "weighty" interest under *Vincent* (after all, almost anything can).[33]

The third and most startling response was voiced by Justice O'Connor in the plurality opinion; that response represents the most resounding defeat for free speech. O'Connor, as did Kennedy, upheld the government's action, but, unlike Kennedy, she did not use the weighted balancing test or subject the government to any form of special scrutiny, strict or intermediate. The government was required to have only a *legitimate* interest and, in this case, its interest in facilitating traffic flow amply satisfied that standard. O'Connor insisted that the state interest need not be "compelling," "significant," "substantial," or "weighty." Instead, she declared that the government action was to be "examined only for reasonableness,"[34] by which she meant only that the government's interest in clearing the sidewalk must be a legitimate or permissible one.

An extended discussion in her opinion about the specific speech activity involved—solicitation—suggests that O'Connor may have distinguished the case before her from *Schneider* on the ground that solicitation is more disruptive of pedestrian traffic flow on the sidewalk than are other speech activities, such as handbilling.[35] I for one doubt the factual predicate of this distinction. It is true, of course, as O'Connor noted, that the pedestrian must stop and think whether to give, but the same could be said of handbilling or even of delivering a speech—the pedestrian may have to stop and think whether to read or listen. But even conceding that solicitation is more disruptive than handbilling, that does not call for adjusting or lowering the standard of review, but only, as Kennedy thought, for concluding that the higher or intermediate standard of review—requiring the state to have a substantial interest—is satisfied. However, the burden of O'Connor's opinion was to disavow the weighted balancing test or any form of special scrutiny, and that ruling turned not on the specific form of the speech activity (solicitation), but rather on the structure of ownership of the underlying property—the sidewalk.

Justice Roberts's perspective on property was functional. He was not concerned with the question of title; in fact, the question of who owned the sidewalk played absolutely no role in his analysis in *Schneider*. Rather, he understood the need of the political activists to reach the public in order to advertise their meeting or present their views, and saw the distributions of handbills on the sidewalk as a perfectly sensible way of achieving that objective. The public used the sidewalk, and the speech activity did not substantially or excessively interfere with the ordinary uses of the physical space in question. Speech was compatible with use.

This functional approach controlled for much of the post-war period, and was largely responsible for the generous protection the Warren Court gave to public demonstrations and protests during the civil rights era. The Justices were always sensitive to the degree of disruption that was being caused—in fact, when the interest in order was weighed against the value of free and open debate, sometimes the Justices were divided over how the balance was to be struck. There was, however, virtually no concern with title. Indeed, in 1968, the Court protected speech activity occurring at a privately owned shopping center on the same terms as it had protected speech activity on state-owned property, such as streets and sidewalks.[36]

In the early 1970s, however, a newly constituted Court broke with this tradition and began to make ownership a central question in its analysis. Under the guise of implementing the state action requirement, the Court closed off private property, including shopping centers and malls, from speech activities.[37] Only government-owned property could be considered a public forum. In a sense, the state had to appear twice: as the agency demanding the silence and as the one enforcing that demand. The Court would begin the weighing process of *Schneider* or the multitiered scrutiny of the later cases only if it were shown that the speech-activity occurred on the property of the state.

At first blush, it would seem that speakers in *Kokinda* could easily meet this new requirement because the sidewalk was constructed and owned by the Postal Service, which may properly be considered a governmental institution. The Postal Service has near-monopoly powers, receives public revenues, and is endowed with many powers of the state. Technically, it operates as a public corporation, rather than as a governmental agency, but the members of its board are appointed by the President. Justice O'Connor did not deny the governmental status of the Postal Service, but chose a different strategy altogether: She chose to disaggregate the state. Almost as though she had fallen captive to the rhetoric of the privatization movement of the Reagan years, O'Connor insisted that in ejecting the political activists the government was acting only its "proprietary capacity," in much the same way as a private business or private landowner might. According to O'Connor, the Postal Service was trying to keep its sidewalk clear in order to facilitate access into a building where it offered various services and products for sale.

Crucial to O'Connor's analysis was a distinction among the various ways the state may act. To support such an approach she cited and quoted a decision of the early 1970s, *Lehman v. Shaker Heights,*[38] where the Court, in an opinion by Justice Blackmun, upheld a municipality's refusal to sell space on its buses for political advertisements. The Court in *Lehman* found that the government was acting in its "commercial capacity" and so was to be judged by a lesser First Amendment standard. To be sure, there is language in *Lehman* supporting the theory disaggregating the state, but the real source of that approach is Justice Rehnquist, who for the last twenty years has argued "that the role of government as sovereign is subject to more stringent limitations than is the role of government as employer, property owner, or educator."[39]

Originally, Rehnquist propounded this theory in lonely dissent. In *Kokinda*, his theory obtained the support of the middle of the Court—not just Justice Scalia and himself, but also Justices White and O'Connor. Then, just two years after *Kokinda,* immediately following the retirement of Justices Brennan and Marshall, the theory disaggregating the state became majority doctrine. This occurred in a case involving terminals in the three major airports in the New York area.[40] Brennan's replacement, David Souter, rejected the theory altogether, insisting that the Court should treat "as a public forum any piece of public property that is 'suitable for discourse' in its physical character, where expressive activity is 'compatible' with the use to which it has actually been put."[41] But Marshall's replacement, Clarence Thomas, joined the four Justices who formed the *Kokinda* plurality, and so there was a majority of five who supported using the disaggregation theory to uphold a ban on solicitation in the terminals.

The airports in question were owned and operated by a governmental agency, the Port Authority. "The terminals are," as Rehnquist, the author of the majority opinion, wrote, "generally accessible to the general public and contain various commercial establishments such as restaurants, snack stands, bars, newsstands, and stores of various types."[42] In a separate concurrence, Justice O'Connor added, "In my view, the Port Authority is operating a shopping mall as well as an airport."[43] Nonetheless, she joined four others—Justices Rehnquist, White, Scalia, and Thomas—to form a majority that refused to subject the Port Authority regulation banning solicitation to strict scrutiny. By way of explanation, Rehnquist wrote, "Where the government is acting as a proprietor, managing its internal operations, rather than acting as lawmaker with the power to regulate or license, its action will not be subjected to the heightened review to which its actions as a lawmaker may be subjected."[44]

In support of this proposition, Rehnquist cited the plurality opinion in *Kokinda* (thus making the circle complete). But he did not offer—in this case or any other—a principled defense of his theory disaggregating the state. Nor is one readily apparent. Of course, the state acts in manifold ways, but that does not mean it is any less the state when it acts in one way or another. Even when the state acts in the guise of employer, property owner, or educator, it remains the instrument of the public and, for that very reason, is given special prerogatives and saddled with special duties, including those that emanate from the Constitution.

To some extent, Rehnquist and O'Connor acknowledged this point, but only to make a marginal concession—namely, recognition that, as O'Connor put it in *Kokinda*, "[t]he Government, even when acting in its proprietary capacity, does not enjoy absolute freedom from First Amendment constraints."[45] The state must have some reason for its action and that reason must be a good one, that is, not one that is illegitimate or forbidden to the state. The question naturally arose as to what reasons are forbidden. In response, O'Connor said that the law must not be "'an effort to suppress expression merely because public officials oppose the speaker's view.'"[46]

This concession echoes the special rules of the categorical approach that apply when the state engages in content regulation, yet the plurality position in *Kokinda* remains troubling. Granted, the Postal Service is under a restraint not applicable to a purely private business, but the restraint is considerably reduced from that applied, for example, to Milwaukee in *Schneider* or even to Los Angeles in *Vincent*. The state need not find a compelling or substantial reason for its action, only a good one. This difference in standards breaks with precedent, and since the state will almost always be able to imagine some permissible reason to defend its action, in practice the more relaxed standard of *Kokinda* deprives the First Amendment of most of its bite.[47] The state cannot defend its action on the ground that it finds the ideas voiced objectionable, but a vast domain of possible justifications still remains available to it.

Viewed in these terms, *Kokinda* represents an especially destructive revision of *Schneider,* even more destructive than *Vincent.* The case stands for the proposition that when government demands silence on its property—and thus is acting in its proprietary capacity—that action will not be subject to the weighted balancing test or any other form of special scrutiny. Fully mindful of what she was doing, O'Connor promised to apply special scrutiny to the action of the government even when it is acting in its "proprietary capacity" if (a) the government property has been "traditionally" open to the public for expressive activity or (b) the government property is "expressly dedicated" to speech activity.[48]

Neither of these two exceptions was available in *Kokinda* itself. The government had allowed solicitation on the sidewalk in the past, but reversed its policy a decade before the confrontation that became the subject of the case arose. Accordingly, O'Connor concluded that the sidewalk was not expressly dedicated to speech activity, and thus the second ex-

ception did not apply. Moreover, although in the past this sidewalk had
been open to the public for expressive activities, it had not always been.
On the basis of this fact, O'Connor held that the requirements of the first
exception—the one couched in terms of traditional practices—had not
been satisfied. Clearly, O'Connor was using an odd definition of the notion of "traditionally"; she interpreted it to mean "always."

The two limitations built into the *Kokinda* rule seem to be a concession
to precedent, or to the honored place the street corner (now understood literally) has held in First Amendment jurisprudence since the days of
Schneider and another of Justice Roberts's opinions, *Hague v. CIO*.[49] It is
difficult, however, to view the exceptions as rooted in a proper understanding of the Constitution. Why should the stringency of the First
Amendment be made to vary according to the traditions of the community
or the decision of the state to dedicate its property expressly for speech
purposes? These exceptions tend to make the Constitution a mechanism
either to codify tradition or to estop the state, but I tend to conceive of the
Constitution in just the opposite way: as a limitation on the prerogatives
of the state and as a basis for critically examining community traditions.

Aside from its theoretical adequacy, a question can also be raised about
the pragmatic significance of these two exceptions to the *Kokinda* rule.
The exceptions may keep the old and familiar street corner open, but they
would leave unprotected all the new configurations of public space—for
example, a government plaza or an airport terminal—and thus make it
more difficult for political activists to reach the public. These days there
are fewer and fewer passersby on the old familiar street corner; the streets
of the city are empty. Granted, a significant portion of the public can be
found in the new downtown mall, or in the suburban shopping centers, especially on a Saturday morning. But since these public arenas are privately owned, more so than the sidewalk of the Postal Service or the terminals of the Port Authority, the principle that lies at the heart of *Kokinda*
puts these places beyond, far beyond, the reach of the First Amendment.
What, then, is left of free speech?

IV

In cases like *Vincent* and *Kokinda*, the Supreme Court has drawn back
from *Schneider* and the decisions of the civil rights era that kept the street
corner free and open. By way of compensation, it affirmed a commitment

to the rule against content regulation. While the majority in *Vincent* only required the state to establish a "substantial" interest, and then gave a weak reading to that requirement, it nonetheless indicated that it would require a "compelling" interest if the state's regulation discriminated on the basis of content. A similar concern for content regulation was espoused in Justice O'Connor's opinion in *Kokinda*: The state can never defend its action on grounds of content or opposition to the speaker's view, even when it is acting in a "proprietary capacity."

Recognition should also be given to the fact that the rule against content regulation has produced some notable free speech victories during the Rehnquist era. Apparently, the state is not encumbered by the rule against content regulation when the state acts in an allocative manner—for example, awarding subsidies[50]—but when the state acts in a regulatory fashion, content-based interventions have not been allowed. The flag burning cases are perhaps the paramount example of this stance.[51] Moreover, the jurisdiction of the censor has remained limited when it comes to the traditional categories of content regulation, such as obscenity, libel, and subversive advocacy.[52]

A question can be raised about whether this protection against content regulation is now as generous as it once was, considering the retirements of Justices Brennan, Marshall, and Blackmun, crucial as they were to the free speech victories of the recent years. An even more fundamental question concerns the sufficiency of the rule against content regulation, for no matter how firm the protection against content regulation may be, and no matter how necessary, I would contend that it is not enough. Protection against access regulations is as integral to a system of free expression as is protection against content regulations.

On several occasions the Supreme Court has declared that under the First Amendment there is no such thing as a false idea.[53] It is the sentiment encapsulated by this declaration that underlies the rule against content regulation and accounts for much of its appeal. No ideas should be excluded from public debate. Access regulations do not brand ideas as false, and thus they avoid this stricture, but they nonetheless have a decisive effect upon the nature of public debate. Such regulations control the opportunities for speech, and by virtue of the fact that not all groups in society have the same speech opportunities, a curtailment of one opportunity—a street corner—may privilege one group over another.

Besides differentially advantaging speakers, access regulations also affect the character of public debate by controlling what the public hears or sees. The most determined citizen can, of course, actively pursue or learn of an idea wherever and however it is expressed—it need only be aired somewhere in society. It would be foolish, however, to take this model— of the citizen running after ideas—as the behavioral norm of our society or of any modern working democracy. A proper regard for democratic values requires easy access to all ideas, for without such access the public is not likely to know its options or the costs of the present arrangements under which it lives.

If a choice need be made between these two free speech rules—one protecting against access regulations and the other against content regulations—I am not clear how that choice should be made or which should be preferred. Conventional wisdom says we should prefer the rule against content regulation. I wonder, however, whether democratic values are indeed furthered by having bold and dramatic rules protecting flag burning or parodies such as those involved in the *Hustler* case—in which a minister confesses to a drunken sexual rendezvous with his mother in an outhouse[54]—while allowing the state to restrict the public's exposure to political discourse of the type involved in *Vincent* and *Kokinda.* Could it be that we have moved one step forward, but two steps back?

While judging the relative significance of these two types of rules may pose a genuine dilemma for democratic theory, fortunately this need not be the Court's burden. There is no inconsistency—logical or otherwise— in generously providing protections against content regulation and against access regulation that impair the public's capacity to be informed of issues of public importance. Indeed, as reference to the civil rights era makes clear, history teaches that both kinds of protections are possible and stem from the same underlying commitment to the enrichment of public debate.

In cases like *Vincent* and *Kokinda* we see the erosion—no, the betrayal—of that very commitment. The present Court speaks of a national commitment to robust public debate, and repeatedly mouths the formula of *New York Times Co. v. Sullivan,* but, as in the media cases, is unprepared to give operative significance to these words. The Court tolerates the silencing hand of the policeman even though he cannot plead a special urgency in defense of his decision to clear the street corner. The present Court does not demand a compelling interest—sometimes it does not even require a substantial one—to justify this suppression of speech. The Court has diluted the standard of review, and, in so doing, seriously compromised the values that lie, as Justice Roberts recognized, "at the foundation of free government by free men."

4

Freedom and Feminism

PROLOGUE

In the mid-1980s, as my work on the Kalven volume was drawing to a close, I began to offer a course on the First Amendment. Building on a seminar that I taught with Alvin Klevorick on the relationship between economic and political power, I focused on cases involving campaign finance, the mass media, and the attempt of political activists to use privately owned property, such as shopping centers, to disseminate their views. Free Speech and Social Structure, *my initial effort to synthesize many of the themes that emerged from the course, naturally focused on these kinds of issues (see Chapter 1).*

In the late 1980s and early 1990s, a number of students in the course began to wonder whether my theory of the First Amendment might be applicable to cases in which inequalities had a social rather than an economic basis. Engaged by the arguments of radical feminists, which were then sweeping the legal academy, they wondered whether the state might have a role in curbing a social institution—pornography—that they saw as an important source of gender inequality. My personal loyalties were sharply divided—I consider both Catharine MacKinnon and Frank Easterbrook, one who spearheaded the campaign against pornography, the other who blocked it, among my favorite students—and the essay that follows is my attempt to come to terms with the new constitutional controversy stirred by feminism. The essay was first presented as a lecture in Rome in October 1991 as part of a conference on feminism and was published in the Georgetown Law Journal *in August 1992.*

Feminism does not belong to the law alone, but during the early 1970s it became a subject of great interest to American lawyers. For participants in the movement, the law was seen both as a domain to be reformed and an instrument of reform. At first, the principal purpose was to create access for women to positions of power that had traditionally been the exclusive province of men, and to eliminate obvious differences in the treatment of men and women. The movement initially propounded a principle banning discrimination and requiring that men and women workers be judged by the same standard. The early 1970s was an age of unisex.

In the late 1970s, two important changes occurred, both largely spearheaded by Catharine MacKinnon. First, there was a shift in the underlying theory of equality, from antidiscrimination to antisubordination. The antidiscrimination principle presupposes a situation where a discrete decisionmaker must award a scarce opportunity to a group of competing individuals. It requires that the selection be based on some functionally related criterion: merit, not gender. In contrast, the antisubordination principle heralded by Mackinnon is more group-oriented. It is concerned not merely with the discriminatory acts of any individual but with any social practice that has the effect of subordinating women, and condemns what is referred to as gender hierarchy.

While the antisubordination principle overlaps with the antidiscrimination principle, it is more extensive, for it recognizes that the social ordering along gender lines is not just the product of arbitrary selection procedures at the individual level. Many social practices and norms are responsible for that ordering, some quite diffuse. For example, in most of society it remains generally expected that women will assume the primary responsibility for the care of children, which in turn has the effect of keeping women at home and restricting their educational and employment opportunities. That social understanding, not attributable to any single decisionmaking authority, may be beyond the reach of the antidiscrimination but not the antisubordination principle, which has been used to criticize that understanding and provide the theoretical basis for state child-care programs and parental leaves.

Second, while the foundational principle of American feminism was shifting in the late 1970s from antidiscrimination to antisubordination, the law paid increasing attention to sexuality. In the early 1970s, feminist lawyers were for the most part critically examining public practices, like admission to universities and job selection. By the end of the decade, however, sexual relationships became increasingly subject to their criticism. The principal concern was with the objectification of women: the transformation of women into sexual objects to be used by men. There was good and sufficient reason to be concerned with objectification in and of itself, since it could be understood as a form of subordination, but feminists such as MacKinnon also saw this practice as having implications beyond the private sphere. Objectification, so it was hypothesized, led men to construct and maintain social practices and values that excluded women from public domains or kept them in inferior positions in employment and education.

This growing concern with objectification, as both a form and cause of inequality, made even the most ordinary heterosexual relationship suspect, but the reform agenda of feminists such as MacKinnon had a more specific focus. MacKinnon's particular targets were sexual harassment in the workplace, prostitution, rape, and pornography. Of all these subjects, the most controversial has been pornography. The campaign against pornography that is linked to her name and that of Andrea Dworkin[1] has divided the feminist movement and alarmed many of its allies.[2] Some have seen the campaign as a diversion of energy, others have objected to it on the ground that it established a new orthodoxy on sexuality, and still others—perhaps the bulk—have objected to it on the ground that it was inconsistent with freedom of speech. In 1985, a federal appeals court held unconstitutional a comprehensive antipornography ordinance drafted by MacKinnon and Dworkin and enacted by Indianapolis, Indiana, the year before.[3]

Campaigns to curb pornography have been commonplace in American history. Most have been based on conservative ideologies or religious sentiments. The one that gave rise to the Indianapolis ordinance differed in that it was predicated upon the egalitarianism that inspires the entire feminist movement. The concern was not the moral offensiveness of sexually explicit images, but with the use of those images to eroticize the subordination of women, the sexual assaults those images may cause, and the coercive processes used to produce and distribute them. Dworkin and MacKinnon presented the Indianapolis ordinance as a civil rights law.

As a civil rights law, the Indianapolis ordinance made claim to the Fourteenth Amendment and its guarantee of equality. It could be seen as a measure to promote equality and thus serve constitutional purposes. Some have defended the Indianapolis ordinance and similar measures on precisely these grounds,[4] but this line of argument did not seem wholly satisfactory. It left us confronting the familiar conflict between liberty and equality, not knowing exactly which one should be given priority. Even if the law furthers equality, it may violate the First Amendment. However, we may be able to resolve the dispute without getting to the conflict of primary principles—the First v. the Fourteenth Amendments, liberty v. equality—but focusing on a different question instead: Was the Indianapolis ordinance in fact a violation of the freedom of speech?

In addressing this issue it is important to avoid the approach of Judge Easterbrook, the author of the court of appeals decision. He treated the ordinance as a single unified whole and struck down the law in its entirety. In fact, the ordinance carefully distinguishes among four offenses and each should have been treated separately. One provision prohibits coercing people to perform in the production of pornography; a second prohibits forcing people to view pornography; a third addresses physical assaults inflicted by someone moved or provoked by a pornographic work; and a fourth prohibits trafficking in pornography.[5] All four offenses share a common enforcement structure—no criminal sanctions, but cease-and-desist orders and damages, issued by an administrative agency and subject to full judicial review. The ordinance contains a strong severability provision,[6] declaring that each provision should stand on its own and be given effect even if another is found invalid. By its very terms, therefore, the ordinance recognizes that different offenses present different First Amendment issues, some more difficult than others, and in my view these differences should have been respected.

I

The least problematic provisions of the ordinance are those that protect against coerced performance in the production of pornography and the forced viewing of pornography. They are predicated on the claim that women are sometimes forced to participate in the production of pornography[7] and that people are sometimes forced to view pornography. The latter is said to occur in a variety of situations ranging from the workplace to the intimacy of the home.

In judging these provisions, I begin with the view, elaborated in earlier chapters, that treats the First Amendment as an instrument of democratic self-governance. Freedom of speech calls for wide and stringent protection for those who speak, or write, or otherwise communicate to the public—protection not just for the words they choose, but also for the means of producing and distributing their speech. State regulations of the means of producing and distributing speech are commonplace, but the First Amendment requires that those regulations not restrict debate unless they advance a sufficiently compelling interest. Imagine, for example, a statute strictly rationing the use of paper to produce political tracts[8] or one aimed at preventing litter which banned all handbilling on public streets.[9] Such measures would be unconstitutional.

There is, however, no comparable danger with the provisions of the Indianapolis ordinance having to do with "coerced performance" or "forced viewing." Like the examples just mentioned, they in fact regulate the means of producing and distributing speech, and as such inevitably have some effect upon public discourse, but the exercise of state power in both instances is strictly limited by the notion of "coercion" or "force." These provisions require that pornography be produced without forced labor and distributed to willing recipients. Through operation of cease-and-desist orders, and as a result of the deterrent effect of liability rules, speech that violates these restrictions would be withdrawn from the public domain. But that is not a loss to be regretted, any more than we regret the loss of speech attributable to rules against plagiarism or copyright infringement. The "forced viewing" and "coerced performance" provisions seek to protect the freedom of performers and the freedom of the audience, and thus tend to reinforce rather than to destroy First Amendment values.

Of course, "coercion" and "force" are terms capable of great expansion and manipulation. But they appear throughout the law, both in common law rules and in statutes, and there is no reason to believe that they are especially lacking integrity when used in this context. As is always the case, they need further limitation and specification,[10] but Judge Easterbrook never gave the state agencies charged with administering the ordinance the chance to develop rules that would provide that limitation. He declared the ordinance invalid on its face. He did not base this preemptive ruling on the expansiveness of the notion of "coercion" or "force," but apparently objected to the partiality of the regulation: Pornography may not be the only form of literature or art where there is "coerced performance" or "forced viewing," yet the legislature only focused on it.[11]

Admittedly, the legislature could have proscribed "coerced performances" in the production of all sexually explicit material, or for that matter, all forms of art or literature, or could have prohibited the "forced viewing" of any film or art. Yet there was ample basis for it to believe that these evils are sufficiently prevalent in the production and distribution of pornography of the type proscribed as to warrant separate and immediate treatment. There is nothing arbitrary about the partiality and it works to the advantage of the First Amendment. The legislature need not burden all speech to address the harms associated specifically with certain types of speech. Of course, as a consequence of the legislative selectivity, films of a sexually explicit nature would be saddled with rules not imposed on other types of films that arguably involve "coerced performance," for example, those films involving torture or violence in a nonsexual setting. But this type of partiality cannot be compared to other forms of partiality that would be impermissible under the First Amendment, such as the state disadvantaging one political candidate or position over another. In the electoral setting, the assumption is that the state can claim no justification for the partiality of its regulation other than the desire to favor one candidate. In the case of the Indianapolis ordinance, the state is trying to protect against coercion in the least intrusive way possible.

II

Similar considerations apply, though perhaps with less force, to the provision of the ordinance regarding pornography that is found to have caused assaults or physical attacks. This aspect of the ordinance is most likely to be involved in situations in which a bizarre sexual crime, for example, a gang rape on a pool table in a barroom, closely tracks an act described and eroticized by a particular work of pornography. Like all the other offenses specified in the ordinance, this one is framed as a prohibition that is enforceable by both cease-and-desist orders and damage awards. A complainant can succeed only upon a showing that there was in fact an assault, and that the assault was directly caused by a pornographic work. In making this showing the complainant will have established a claim for damages. After liability is established, a cease-and-desist order might be also issued, but the damage award and the prospect of other claims would effectively discourage any further circulation and make the cease-and-desist order unnecessary or of only marginal importance.

At first glance, it would seem that this provision of the ordinance could be squared with the First Amendment on the theory that it treats works that cause sexual assaults as though they are incitements to violence. First Amendment doctrine allows the state to punish both the rioter and the person who incited the riot. This theory is a troubling one, however, because we can never be certain as to which utterances might constitute an incitement. We fear that by imposing liability upon someone for speech that is shown to be an incitement, we might discourage speech that does not constitute an incitement and that should not be discouraged. The danger of this chilling effect—deterring what should not be deterred—is manifest when criminal sanctions are threatened, but it is also present when there is a risk that damages will be awarded. Indeed, in the libel area we recognize that allowing a person to recover damages for an injury to reputation from false statements might chill or discourage the press from quite proper and important reportage or comment.[12] Similarly, there is reason to fear that allowing a victim of a rape or physical assault to recover damages from the publisher of a magazine or producer of a film that led to a sexual attack might dangerously chill or discourage all kinds of publications or films, many of which are essential for free and open debate on issues of public importance.

The risk of this chill cannot be denied. Yet we learned to cope with it in other branches of the law, including libel, recognizing that it is a price that must be paid in order to accommodate conflicting values. A similar attitude seems appropriate here. The Court's response to the possible chill of libel laws was not to transform the First Amendment into a blanket prohibition against such laws; rather the Court acted more circumspectly. First, it barred criminal laws against libel of public officials.[13] Second, it created specific limitations to the cause of action for damages, for example, by requiring proof that a speaker knew or had reason to know what was said was false.[14] In a similar spirit, the system of accountability established by the Indianapolis ordinance seeks to minimize the risk of a chilling effect. There is no criminal liability, only a right to sue for damages, and the person seeking to recover damages is required to show that (1) there was a "direct" causal relation between the assault and the pornography; (2) the assault was tied to some "specific" pornographic work; and (3) the defendant knew or had reason to know that the work met the statutory definition of pornography.[15]

Clearly, the Indianapolis City Council might have done more to minimize the chilling effect. For example, it could have increased plaintiff's evidentiary burden from the "preponderance of the evidence" standard customarily found in civil cases to require a more demanding "clear and convincing" demonstration of the direct causal link between the assault and the pornography. Or it could have required proof that the defendant intended or wanted such an attack to occur, or was recklessly indifferent to whether it might occur. As enacted, the ordinance requires the defendant in a damage action to have known that the work met the statutory definition of pornography, but it does not require a linkage between the intention or desires of the defendant and the sexual assault. The incitement analogy would seem to suggest such a linkage, but linkage in that context may stem from the scienter requirement of the criminal law; it is not needed in a civil action or imposed by the First Amendment.

The judgment of whether these additional safeguards are needed depends on a nuanced assessment of the risk of a chilling effect juxtaposed against the need to prevent sexual assault. As with the limiting rules surrounding the use of terms like "coercion" and "force," some of these safeguards might have been developed on a case-by-case basis as the ordinance was applied over time. But, once again, Judge Easterbrook was too impatient for that: Striking down the ordinance before it was ever applied, he denied the courts the opportunity so effectively used in the libel context to seek an accommodation of conflicting values by crafting additional safeguards in the process of administering the statute. He objected to the system of accountability itself, complaining that the definition of pornography upon which it rested made actionable only those works that advanced a certain viewpoint regarding women, specifically, the view that women are sexual objects to be used by men.[16] Pornography was defined in the ordinance as the "sexually explicit subordination of women,"[17] and the system of accountability was thus limited to that which embodied or advanced such a view of women. Judge Easterbrook saw this as a forbidden instance of viewpoint discrimination.[18]

Like every law, the Indianapolis ordinance promotes a viewpoint, specifically the view that women should not be subordinated and should not be subject to physical violence. It also exposes films and productions which embody or express a contrary view to a system of accountability for the assaults that might result from the expression of that viewpoint. As with the "coerced performance" or "forced viewing" provisions, a certain genre of literature or art—that which is sexually explicit and subordinates women—is subjected to possible sanctions that others are not. For example, there is no system of accountability for works that cause physical harm to, or otherwise promote the subordination of, other groups (e.g., blacks or Jews), regardless of whether these works are sexually explicit. Nor is there a system of accountability for sexual assaults on women that might somehow be triggered by sexually explicit works that celebrate the power of women or that view women on equal terms.

However, these limits on the system of accountability do not strike me as fatal. The legislators may well have decided that the likelihood of an assault triggered by films or magazines is far greater for women than other groups. Other disadvantaged groups may be subjected to what is euphemistically called "hate speech" today, but they do not confront the level of exposure presented by the pornography industry.[19] Moreover, as to sexually explicit works that present women on equal terms, the legislature was surely entitled to take the position that the risk of physical violence triggered by such works is far less than for works depicting the subordination of women, and that it does not justify regulation.

These are the kind of judgments that legislators make all the time, and it is hard to see why the First Amendment denies them the opportunity to do so here. The Indianapolis City Council could have created a system of accountability for all physical assaults directly caused by a film or magazine; in that instance, the analogy to the law imposing liability for libel or incitement to violence would be stronger. But the First Amendment would not be served by requiring a system of such total regulation, for it would considerably broaden the risk of a chilling effect. In that sense, the partiality of the regulation serves First Amendment values rather than interferes with them. The partiality of the regulation may skew public debate by heightening the risks associated with the production of one art form. But disadvantaging one, though only one, form of art that leads to violent victimization imposes little distortion on the democratic process and at the same time is narrowly tailored to protect women from severe injuries.

In another branch of First Amendment law, one concerning the regulation of public fora, the Supreme Court has developed a body of decisions that condemns viewpoint discrimination and that might be thought to lend support to Judge Easterbrook's position.[20] Imagine a street corner with two speakers holding forth—one in favor of a war, one opposing it. The decisions in question deny the state the power to discriminate or choose between these speakers—to arrest one speaker, but not the other. One can well understand the power of the principle against viewpoint discrimination in the imagined context, but that principle has only limited applicability to the system of accountability enacted by the Indianapolis City Council.

To begin with, one should note that the norm against viewpoint discrimination, like any antidiscrimination rule, does not forbid all distinctions but only unjustified ones. The state cannot choose between two speakers on the street corner on the ground that it would like to hear one viewpoint discussed rather than the other. That would be an impermissible distortion of public debate. It can, however, arrest one of the speakers on the ground that he or she is inciting a riot. Similarly, while the system of accountability established by the Indianapolis ordinance distinguishes between two viewpoints that may be furthered by sexually explicit work—women as equal versus women as subordinate—that difference of treatment can be justified on the ground that one type of work is more likely than the other to provoke physical assaults. There is ample evidence indicating that this was the reasoning that led the members of the City Council to limit the system of accountability as they did,[21] but their intent is not controlling. In judging the action of the police officer who arrests the speaker, what is crucial is not the actual motivation for choosing between speakers, but whether an independent objective basis exists for that choice. In this case, the proper inquiry is whether there is a basis for distinguishing between these speakers because one, but not the other, is likely to lead to sexual violence, a harm the state may validly seek to prevent.

Public forum cases not only permit the state to choose among speakers, provided the distinction is not based on a judgment about the merits of the idea being expressed, but they also bear witness to a general First Amendment rule that allows state regulations that have the effect of stopping or discouraging speech. As these cases indicate, the First Amendment docs not act as an impenetrable shield around a speaker, even one holding forth in a public forum, but rather forces the state to bear the burden of giving an especially urgent or weighty justification—a compelling one—for any regulation that has a silencing effect. Annoying pedestrians is not enough of a justification, but preventing a riot is. The Indianapolis system of accountability would have a silencing effect, but surely Indianapolis has a compelling interest in deterring sexual attacks and compensating victims. Indianapolis might have been content to hold responsible only those individuals who engaged in the physical attack, but there are considerable advantages—arguably compelling ones—for going further back in the causal sequence. Most important, doing so makes it less likely that the attack will ever occur; it operates as a double check and makes the prospect of a damage recovery more realistic.

III

This leaves for consideration the trafficking provision of the Indianapolis ordinance, which I have saved for last because it presents the greatest challenge to freedom of speech. Unlike the "physical assault" provision, it is not aimed at the consequences of the published material, and unlike the "coerced performance" and "forced viewing" provisions, it is not limited to means of production or distribution that are coercive, but rather it seeks to stop all production and distribution of such material. The offense consists of the production and distribution of the material itself, not the consequences it might produce, nor the coercion used in its production or distribution; for that reason, the tension with the First Amendment is most acute.

This tension is acknowledged in the ordinance itself. The ordinance defines pornography in general terms as "the graphic sexually explicit subordination of women," and then identifies six different categories of material.[22] The offenses of "physical assault," "coerced performance," or "forced viewing" could involve material from any of the six categories, including the last, which seems aimed at so-called soft-core pornography of the *Playboy* or *Penthouse* variety: "Women are presented as sexual objects for domination, conquest, violation, exploitation, possession, or use, or through postures or positions of servility or submission or display."[23] This last category of publication, however, is beyond the reach of the trafficking offense. That provision applies only to the most violent and brutal forms of pornography, which are described by the other five categories. Category (2), for instance, consists of material that presents women "as sexual objects who experience sexual pleasure in being raped."[24] Category (3) consists of material that presents women "as sexual objects tied up or cut up or mutilated."[25]

This limitation on the trafficking offense—removing soft-core pornography from its reach—decreases its likely efficacy. As I said, feminists do not attack pornography because it is shocking or indecent, but rather because it works to perpetuate the subordination of women. The underlying premise of such regulation is that pornography leads men to form a powerful association between sexual arousal and female subordination, and thus creates and sustains barriers to women's equality that are rooted in male sexual identity.[26] There is a question, at least in my mind, as to whether the feminist campaign against pornography is premised on an overvaluation of the role of such material as a key determinant in the socialization process of men and the formation of their sexual identity, and those doubts grow insofar as the attack becomes confined to the more extreme categories of pornography. My hunch is that brutal magazines or films of the type covered by the trafficking offense play a negligible role in our culture, and in the socialization of most men or in the formation of their personalities.[27] This does not mean that the ban on trafficking is unjustified, but only that the justification is more attenuated than might first appear. Curb the more brutal and shocking forms of pornography and that will lessen the demand for all types of pornography, even the softer variety, and also redefine the norms of what is permissible to punish.

While narrowing the focus of the trafficking offense lessens its likely contribution to the achievement of equality, it also lessens the force of the First Amendment objection. Seen in its proper form, the question posed is whether the First Amendment protects the production and distribution of sexually explicit material that presents women as sexual objects who, for example, enjoy sexual pleasure when being raped. This kind of material hardly seems central to democratic debate and in fact seems included within that larger category of material—"obscenity"—that the Supreme Court has routinely allowed to be curtailed, even by threat of criminal prosecution.

Judge Easterbrook noted in his opinion that the definition of pornography in the ordinance did not meet the criteria that the Supreme Court laid down in *Miller v. California*[28] to mark the outer bounds of obscenity censorship. According to that case, the material must (1) appeal to a prurient interest in sex, (2) portray sexual activity in a patently offensive way, and (3) lack serious social, aesthetic, or political value.[29] Judge Easterbrook was entirely correct in noting that the Indianapolis ordinance did not use the *Miller* formula to define the proscribed material. But, unlike him, I do not believe this omission justified invalidating the trafficking provision in the preemptive way that he did.

First of all, the *Miller* constitutional definition of obscenity has been used by the Supreme Court on a case-by-case basis to determine whether some particular criminal prosecution or civil interdiction could stand. There is no requirement that the state statute or local ordinance itself incorporate, in so many words, the *Miller* definition. In fact, most of the state and municipal obscenity statutes that have come before the Court have had no definitions of obscenity whatsoever, and a Court did not respond to this omission by invalidating those laws. Even when it found a regulation to reach beyond the limits set by the *Miller* test, it left the statute standing but limited its scope of applicability. For example, in 1966 the Supreme Court set aside Massachusetts's attempt to censor the book *Fanny Hill* on the ground that the material lacked one of the requisite elements of the constitutional definition of obscenity, but the Court did not invalidate the state statute.[30] A similar method could have been applied to the Indianapolis ordinance: A court could have waited to see whether the banned material actually met the constitutional definition of obscenity. It would be hard to imagine material falling within the trafficking offense that would not be patently offensive or would not appeal to a

prurient interest in sex, and even though the ordinance was not self-limit-
ing, a judge could have waited, as the Court did with *Fanny Hill*, to see
whether the particular work in question had serious political or aesthetic
value.

Moreover, in passing a new legislative program, such as that represented by the Indianapolis ordinance, there was no need to assume that the
Supreme Court's current definition of obscenity—the so-called *Miller*
test—is the only possible test for identifying sexually explicit material
that is censorable. At the moment there is a settled quality to the *Miller*
test, but in truth it is a relatively recent creation. The Court's definition of
obscenity was first suggested in a 1957 decision,[31] evolved during the
1960s,[32] and then received yet another reformulation in *Miller* in 1973.[33]
The *Miller* definition is but a gloss upon the First Amendment, trying to
accommodate three different considerations: (1) an appreciation of the
dangers to social norms and even to physical well-being that obscenity arguably presents; (2) respect for the original intent of the First Amendment,
on the theory that the Framers did not think that by protecting "the freedom of speech" they were protecting free circulation of obscene publications; and (3) a commitment to broaden the gambit of public discourse as
a way of furthering democratic values. The *Miller* definition might be
taken to represent a sensible accommodation of these conflicting concerns, yet there is no reason to believe that it is the only possible accommodation, or that it should preclude other efforts. In fact, the Supreme
Court has itself reformulated the constitutional bounds of state power to
interfere with speech when it has dealt with sexually explicit material depicting or aimed at children,[34] or material that is carried over the public
airways.[35] The Indianapolis ordinance invited another reformulation, in
the service of another worthy cause: sexual equality.

In objecting to the trafficking provisions of the Indianapolis ordinance,
Judge Easterbrook again complained not only of the fact that the definition of pornography in the ordinance was not coextensive with the *Miller*
test, but also that it was viewpoint-specific:[36] Pornography is defined not
simply in terms of sexual explicitness, but also requires the subordination
of women, for example, the depiction of women as sexual objects who experience sexual pleasure in being raped, cut up, or mutilated. A work that
is sexually explicit but expresses a revulsion toward such horrors would
not be covered. While the trafficking provision of the Indianapolis ordinance was in that sense indeed viewpoint-specific, this consideration did
not have to preclude it from constitutionally being applied to a work that
otherwise met the *Miller* test.

All obscenity ordinances seek to further some particular viewpoint—for example, about the proper attitude toward sexual behavior or what kind of sexual activity should be publicly displayed—and are allowed to stand, notwithstanding the ban against viewpoint discrimination, because they are based not on disagreement over the idea expressed but on the harm to social norms or values that would be occasioned by the distribution of the material. Most traditional obscenity statutes are not viewpoint-specific, but imagine an obscenity ordinance specifically aimed at sexually explicit films that eroticize sodomy and present it as a highly pleasurable form of sexual activity. Presumably, its viewpoint specificity would not prevent that ordinance from being constitutionally applied to a film that otherwise met the *Miller* criteria. The film could be banned if it appealed to a prurient interest in sex, was patently offensive, and was without serious aesthetic or political value. Similarly, the fact that the Indianapolis ordinance defines the limits of the offense in terms of a specific viewpoint—that it is wrong to present women as sexual objects who enjoy rape—would not put it outside the bounds the Supreme Court has established for obscenity regulation.[37]

Recently, the Supreme Court issued a stern warning against the state using the broad power it has over a so-called unprotected category of speech to favor one side in a political debate.[38] The case in question involved "fighting words," not obscenity, but Justice Scalia, writing for the majority, repeatedly used an example from the obscenity field to argue his position. He thought there was no difference between using a partial or selective ban on "fighting words" to advance the cause of tolerance and manipulating the "obscenity" exception to stifle criticism of government. He took as his starting point the proposition that it would be unconstitutional to "enact an ordinance prohibiting only those legally obscene works that contain criticism of the city government or, indeed, that do not include endorsement of the city government."[39]

It may seem that the Indianapolis trafficking provision runs afoul of Justice Scalia's stricture since that provision is linked to the cause of equality: Only those images or words that subordinate women or somehow promote their subordination, as opposed to their elevation or equal treatment, are proscribed. But Justice Scalia made clear that he was not proscribing all selective regulations, nor even those that embody a content discrimination, but only those in which, as in the obscenity–city government example he used, the content discrimination was unrelated to the "distinctively proscribable content" of the speech.[40] He was complaining of extraneous content discrimination.

Justice Scalia's hostility toward content discrimination is based on the fear that it tends to "drive certain ideas or viewpoints from the marketplace,"[41] but he did not see such a danger when the content discrimination that defines the selective regulation is related to the reasons why the state is allowed to regulate the category of speech in the first place.[42] Accordingly, he acknowledged that the federal government could choose to criminalize only those threats of violence that are directed against the President, since, as he wrote, "[T]he reasons why threats of violence are outside the First Amendment (protecting individuals from the fear of violence, from the disruption that fear engenders, and from the possibility that the threatened violence will occur) have special force when applied to the person of the President."[43] Similarly, while the trafficking ban does indeed single out certain sexually explicit images or material, specifically those that subordinate women, the reason for that selection is closely related to one of the reasons why obscenity is proscribable in the first place: to protect women from violence and sexual abuse.[44]

Thus far I have suggested, contrary to Judge Easterbrook's opinion, that the trafficking provision of the Indianapolis ordinance is consistent with the Supreme Court's stance on obscenity. At the most, one can say that some applications of the Indianapolis ordinance might be prohibited, depending upon, first, the specific nature of the material, and second, the specific limits placed on the state under the *Miller* test or some variant of it. If the Supreme Court's position is still good law, then the trafficking provision of the Indianapolis ordinance should have been allowed to stand, though with limits applied to it on a case-by-case basis. A deeper objection to the trafficking provision comes from those who have serious misgivings about obscenity regulations in general. This group includes a good portion of the liberal community, including many who strongly support the feminist movement. They doubt the validity of the trafficking provision of the Indianapolis ordinance not because it conflicts with what the Supreme Court has said is permissible in regulating sexually explicit material, but rather because they believe that the Court's willingness to tolerate obscenity regulation is itself a serious compromise of the commitment to protect the freedom of speech.

One branch of this critique of obscenity regulation strikes me as unpersuasive. It is libertarian in nature, and decries the Indianapolis trafficking provision and all other obscenity statutes on the grounds that such laws interfere with the freedom of artists, writers, and publishers to convey their views and ideas to the public. These critics view the First Amendment as a protection of individual autonomy: a freedom to speak, to say whatever one wishes. To me, however, such an interpretation of the First

Amendment is unappealing either as a rule of law or as a philosophic principle, for no reason is given to prefer the autonomy of the speaker over that of those who might be harmed or offended by the speech. Filmmakers treasure the freedom to make the kinds of films they wish, and writers and publishers are equally insistent on their freedom. But it is not clear why their freedom should be given priority over the freedom that other people have to control the kinds of works they are exposed to or the kind of environment in which they live.

A second critique of the Supreme Court's obscenity doctrine—one associated with the work of Alexander Meiklejohn,[45] and more persuasive to me—sees the First Amendment more as an instrument of collective self-governance than of individual autonomy. It casts the underlying theory of the First Amendment in democratic terms, as a way of ensuring the essential precondition for popular deliberation and choice—robust public debate. Obviously, speech that specifically addresses some question of government policy has an immediate and direct claim to protection under this theory of free speech. But art and literature, even that which makes no mention of politics and government affairs, is also protected. As Meiklejohn insisted, "I believe, as a teacher, that the people do need novels and dramas and paintings and poems 'because they will be called upon to vote.' "[46] Art, all art, even the sexually explicit, can be politically valuable and as such is most assuredly part of what I have referred to as public debate—that sphere of human activity that the First Amendment seeks to protect and enlarge.

Traditional measures to suppress sexually explicit material threaten to curtail and diminish the robustness of public debate without offering a countervalue comparable to that underlying laws prohibiting incitements to violence or making libel actionable, and thus should be viewed with great suspicion. The same danger to free speech is presented by the trafficking provision of the Indianapolis ordinance, even though it has a narrower compass than the typical obscenity regulation. The ordinance seeks among other things to interdict sexually explicit works of art or literature that portray women as experiencing sexual pleasure during rape. Rape is horrible and is to be condemned in the most emphatic way. Yet under the doctrine favoring robust public debate, this law regulating the expression of views about, or depiction of, rape should be no more acceptable than a law that banned trafficking in works of art or literature that extolled the pleasures or desirability of adultery or sadomasochism.

Some may see a difference between rape, on the one hand, and adultery or sadomasochism, on the other, inasmuch as the raped woman is an involuntary victim of a criminal attack, while participation in adultery or sadomasochism is presumably both consensual and generally legal. It is also true that rape and the fear of rape, unlike adultery and perhaps also sadomasochism, perpetuate the subordination of a disadvantaged group and thus offend the egalitarian aspirations of the Constitution understood in the most general terms. All this might be acknowledged, yet it does not require a different result under the First Amendment. Democracy requires that all laws, including the constitutional guarantee of equality, always be open to reconsideration, revision, and repeal. I emphatically reject the notion—made famous in our time by Robert Bork[47]—that the First Amendment leaves unprotected advocacy of unlawful or even unconstitutional conduct. To borrow a formulation from the Supreme Court, under the First Amendment there is no such thing as a false idea.[48]

This view of the First Amendment does not leave the state powerless. The state is of course free to outlaw the undesirable conduct advocated, and all incitements to unlawful action. For example, while the state may not prohibit the general advocacy of the violent overthrow of government, it is certainly free to make it a crime to violently overthrow the government, or, more significantly, to incite others to engage in that conduct.[49] Incitement occurs when individuals are being urged to engage in the proscribed conduct and the matter has passed beyond the deliberative sphere. There is no more room for speech.

Indianapolis may have been exercising this well-recognized state prerogative when it provided for damages for someone assaulted as the direct result of a specific pornographic work. Conceivably, the trafficking provision could also be understood as a means to curb incitements to violence. Insofar as it is backed by a damage remedy, it may discourage speech that incites violence. It may, however, be extremely difficult to measure damages, since the violence has not yet occurred when the statute is enforced, and as a result the trafficking offense is likely to be enforced only through cease-and-desist orders. Even then, the incitement theory would require, on a case-by-case basis, a showing that the speech passed beyond the general advocacy of an idea to an actual incitement of imminent illegal conduct. In the case of printed material, this is a difficult standard to meet, though perhaps less so with films.

The state might also have the right to stop the general advocacy of an idea when that advocacy has the effect of interfering with the speech rights of others. In that instance, the state ban on speech does not restrict or impoverish public debate, but paradoxically enough, broadens it, for it allows all voices to be heard. The state acts not as a censor, but rather as a parliamentarian, requiring some to shut up so others can speak. Arguably, the trafficking provision of the Indianapolis ordinance could be justified on the ground that pornography silences women.[50] But once again, to avoid unleashing a general censorial power, one must be careful to delineate two different kinds of silencing dynamics.

One is ideational. It is derived solely from the content of the message. Pornography, especially of the type that is the subject of the trafficking provision, may be understood as a demand or plea that women be silent, or somehow be silenced through violence. It is as though the pornographer said "women should not speak" or "women should not be taken seriously." A question can be raised as to whether pornography, even of the brutal kind covered by the trafficking provision, can be reduced to, or can be said to promote, this idea. But even if pornography can be understood in this way, I am wary of using the idea alone as a predicate for state regulation. My reluctance stems in part from doubt that the plea or demand for women's silence is, in itself, effective. Saying something does not make it so. I also fear that the recognition of such a silencing dynamic would remove from public discourse a whole category of ideas, namely, those that demand that various people be silenced or kept in silence ("Kill the Jews," "Reinstate Slavery," "Establish a Dictatorship of the Proletariat"). Life on this planet would be significantly better without these ideas in circulation, but allowing the state to ban them would give it the power to determine which ideas should enter or become part of public debate, a power that is inconsistent with the value entrusted to the First Amendment—popular sovereignty.

The second silencing dynamic is sociological. It is concerned not just with the idea itself ("women should be silenced"), but with the conditions and circumstances under which the idea is circulated and distributed. It complains not of de Sade, or of the writing of a book, or the making of a film that eroticizes rape, but of the industrial dimensions of pornography: the constant bombardment in our culture of books, magazines, and films that propound this idea. It is not any particular work of art or literature that is the source of concern, but rather the fact that women know that in any place—Indianapolis, New York, or Rome—there is a flood of books, magazines, films, or video cassettes that present them as sexual objects who experience sexual pleasure in being raped, cut up, or mutilated. It is this social practice, rather than any particular book, magazine, or film, that induces fear in women and inculcates in them the habit of silence, or that leads men not to listen to what women say or not to take them seriously;

and it is this social practice that impoverishes public debate and gives substance to Catharine MacKinnon's rage: "We are stripped of authority and
reduced and devalidated and silenced."[51]

Many factors account for the silencing of women. All the fault does not
lie with the pornography industry, even less with the especially brutal kind
of pornography covered by the trafficking ban. One can only wonder how
much of this material is in circulation, taking its toll on the consciousness
of men and women or otherwise shaping our culture. But there is nothing
in the Constitution that precludes a legislative body from deciding that the
silencing of women occasioned by the circulation of this kind of material
is of sufficient magnitude to justify an attempt at regulation. Once again,
this is a matter that can well be trusted to legislative judgment.[52]

There is a tradition in First Amendment cases of the judiciary making
an independent assessment of the facts that are offered in support of an
order stopping the circulation of a publication or film. This practice—
most pronounced during the Warren Court's administration of its obscenity doctrine[53]—stems from the special significance attributed to speech,
lying as it does at the heart of our democratic system. Such special
scrutiny is not wholly appropriate in the context of the Indianapolis ordinance, however, for speech appears as both the object and justification of
regulation; the speech of those producing and distributing pornographic
material is restricted in order to enhance the speech of women. Under
these circumstances, a highly skeptical attitude toward legislative judgments of fact might work against the preferred freedom.

However, even if legislators are granted a measure of deference, there
is no denying that the theory I have outlined for sustaining various applications of the trafficking ban as a protection of speech would tax the imag-
inative and temporal resources of the judiciary. The narrow technical
question before the court in each instance would be whether the film or
publication met the definition of pornography set forth in the ordinance.
But in order to meet the requirements of the First Amendment, the judge
would have to make some assessment of the entire environment of which
the challenged material was a part in order to determine whether it had the
effect of silencing women, or more precisely, whether the legislature had
good reason for believing that it had that effect. Are women speaking and
being heard? Are they being silenced or discredited by the pornography
industry? What contribution does the targeted work make to the power of
that industry? Does the targeted work present some unique perspective
that must be protected in order to avoid the suppression of an idea?

These inquiries, and all the others that might be required to operationalize the silencing theory, are highly context-dependent and broad-ranging, but they are not at all alien to free speech jurisprudence. They are foreshadowed by the third branch of the *Miller* test making the protection of speech dependent on whether a work of art has serious political or aesthetic value. To take an example from another branch of the law, comparable sociological inquiries are required by the test that conditions interdiction of subversive advocacy upon a showing of a clear and present danger. This is especially true if, as Learned Hand insisted in the communist conspiracy cases, the judge is to take account of both the gravity of the danger and the probability of it materializing.[54] Moreover, however burdensome such inquiries might be, they may be justified by the value they serve—strengthening democratic debate. The purpose of the law is not to make judging easy, but to make sure that justice is done.

The Indianapolis ordinance as a whole is rooted in a concern for equality, and so is the trafficking ban. It is not based on a distaste or revulsion for the kind of brutal pornography that it reaches, though that is surely present, but aspires to make some small contribution to eradicating the social dynamics that result in the subordination of women. Simply to offer equality—taken as a Fourteenth Amendment value—as a defense for the trafficking regulation will not meet the free speech objection, unless we somehow postulate a priority for equality. However, once we understand that equality need not be seen as an independent value, based solely on the Fourteenth Amendment, but rather that it has First Amendment dimensions as well, the constitutional issue presented by the trafficking provision appears in a wholly new light. Democracy requires that everyone have an equal chance to speak and to be heard. The trafficking provision, aimed as it is at the pornography industry in its most extreme form, should be seen as a friend rather than an enemy of democracy: an effort to establish the preconditions for free and open debate.

5

State Activism and State Censorship

PROLOGUE

Can the state ever be a friend of freedom? This is the central question that concerned me in the free speech course I offered at Yale and in the essays presented earlier in this volume. For the most part, the question has been posed in a conventional context, in which the state acts in a regulatory manner, much like a policeman. Early on, I acknowledged that the state makes important contributions to political freedom when it acts affirmatively, say by providing public education and public libraries. Yet there was not much Supreme Court case law on the subject, and as a result, this facet of state activity tended to get slighted in the classroom and in my writing.

Then, in 1989, a tremendous public controversy erupted over the decision of the National Endowment for the Arts (NEA) to fund an exhibition of the photographs of Robert Mapplethorpe. It yielded no Supreme Court decision but resulted in an obscenity prosecution, a presidential commission, and several rounds of congressional legislation, one of which created a new governing structure for the NEA. The Mapplethorpe exhibition, which raised issues that are still a matter of public controversy, provided me with a wonderful medium for exploring many of the free speech problems posed by the affirmative state.

I first viewed the Mapplethorpe exhibition in the Wadsworth Athenaeum in Hartford, Connecticut, in the fall of 1989. As I left the exhibition, I thought I finally understood the social dynamics that led America to engage in an act that is now unthinkable—censoring James Joyce's Ulysses. *I also realized that to explore successfully those dynamics in class, I would need to recreate the exhibition. With the help of two of my students, Elizabeth E. deGracia and Donald W. Hawthorne, I presented the exhibition on slides to my class in the spring of 1990 and again in the spring of 1991, just as this essay appeared in the* Yale Law Journal.

Prior to publication, I shared a draft of this essay with a group of lawyers and philosophers—known as SELF (Society of Ethical and Legal Philosophy)—to which I had belonged for some years. In fact, drafts of almost all the essays in this book have benefited from discussions with that group. This particular essay especially provoked one member of the group—Charles Fried—and eventually led to an important critical essay of his, Speech in the Welfare State, *which was published by the* University of Chicago Law Review *in 1992.*

The First Amendment has been used most successfully in keeping the criminal law at bay. Indeed, the free speech tradition principally evolved in cases in which individuals were prosecuted for a number of different crimes—disturbing the peace, inciting a riot, interfering with the draft, conspiring to overthrow the government, seditious libel, or distributing obscene material. As the story is told, the Supreme Court first erred on the side of the censor, allowing convictions on such charges to stand, but starting in the 1930s the Court began to place decisive limits on such uses of the police power. Under established doctrine, the state is sometimes allowed to arrest and prosecute speakers—freedom of speech is not absolute—but that is supposed to be a most extraordinary occurrence.

In recent years we have come to understand that the state does not act just as policeman, but also as educator, employer, landlord, librarian, broadcaster, banker, and patron of the arts. The twentieth century has witnessed an enormous growth of state power and, even more, a proliferation of the ways in which this power has come to be exercised. In speaking of the rise of the activist state in America, we refer not simply to the quantitative growth of state intervention, but more importantly to the changes in the ways that the state has intervened: a movement from negative to affirmative modalities. This development has been of considerable importance politically and socially and, at the same time, has created new challenges for the First Amendment. Is it an infringement of freedom of speech for a public library to exclude from its shelves certain radical books? Or for a public school to offer a course on evolution but not creationism? Or for a state-owned television station to promote the development of nuclear power and not provide an opportunity for environmental groups to voice their opposition?

In grappling with these questions, the Supreme Court has acknowledged that the First Amendment applies to affirmative as well as negative modes of state power, but it has encountered great difficulty in specifying exactly *how* it applies. In the most general terms, the question is whether the Court should apply a double standard—should the Court be more lax in its review of affirmative exercises of power than it is when it reviews the enforcement of the criminal law? This is the question I wish to address, and to do so I will focus on the constitutional and political controversy concerning Robert Mapplethorpe and the National Endowment for the Arts (NEA). The dispute was spurred by a number of public statements by Senator Jesse Helms of North Carolina objecting to the use of public funds to support the show. Although it did not reach the Supreme Court, for more than a year the Mapplethorpe controversy was a matter of national importance. It was in the newspapers almost on a daily basis; it resulted in one criminal prosecution, the appointment of a presidential commission, and several rounds of legislation; and it raised complex issues that every modern democracy must confront in adjusting to the changes in the way state power is exercised.

I

Robert Mapplethorpe was a successful New York photographer. He was gay and in March 1989 died of AIDS. At that time, he was forty-two years old. Shortly before his death, a retrospective exhibition of his photographs was organized by the Institute for Contemporary Art of the University of Pennsylvania. That exhibition consisted of 175 photographs, the subjects of which varied widely. A number of the photographs were portraits of Mapplethorpe himself and of celebrity friends such as Andy Warhol; others portrayed flowers (lilies or tulips), which were presented in almost sculptural form, as if hewn from cold, inanimate stone. There were also two photographs of children of some of Mapplethorpe's friends: One was of a naked boy, sitting on the back of a chair; another was of a young girl, with her dress raised. She is not wearing undergarments. Still another group of photographs consisted of shots of the male body, often heads, but sometimes the naked torso or its various parts. They too appeared sculptural. One photograph in this group, entitled "Man in Polyester Suit," was of a black man dressed in an inexpensive suit of clothing with his penis exposed. The top of his body, from the shoulders up, and the bottom, from the knees down, are cropped. A final group of photographs—perhaps the most provocative—depicted homosexual relationships and homosexual activity. In one, two men are kissing ("Larry and Bobby Kissing") and in another, entitled "Embrace," two young men—one black, the other white, both wearing jeans, naked to their waists—are affectionately embracing one another. In addition, a number of photographs, part of the so-called X, Y, Z Series, include depictions of sexual activity that could be considered sadomasochistic.[1]

Starting in the early part of 1989 and continuing through the fall of 1990, the show was exhibited in various museums throughout the country. In one locality—Cincinnati, Ohio—a museum and its director were prosecuted for violating a local criminal statute that prohibits the pandering of obscenity.[2] The director faced a fine of up to $2,000 and a one-year jail sentence if convicted; the museum faced a $10,000 fine. The indictment was filed in the spring of 1990, soon after the opening of the show there, and later that fall, after a highly publicized trial lasting several weeks, the jury voted to acquit. As with any jury decision, it is impossible to know exactly what that verdict turned on—a dislike of the prosecutor? a failure of proof? a belief that pictures are constitutionally protected? a concern for the reputation of Cincinnati? It seems relatively clear, however, that the prosecution could not have survived under established First Amendment doctrine and that the jury would have been reversed if it had decided differently.

In the obscenity context, the Supreme Court's strategy has been to limit state censorship by propounding a constitutional definition of obscenity to demarcate the outer boundary of state power: Material that does not fall within the narrow parameters of the constitutional definition of obscenity is protected. This strategy, first announced in 1957 in *Roth v. United States*,[3] evolved through the 1960s in cases like the one involving *Fanny Hill*,[4] and received its most recent statement in 1973 in *Miller v. California*.[5] As noted in the previous chapter, *Miller* provides that a conviction for distributing or publishing allegedly obscene material will be allowed to stand if, and only if, the material, taken as a whole, (1) appeals to a prurient interest in sex,[6] (2) depicts sexual activity in a patently offensive way, and (3) is without serious aesthetic, political, or scientific value.

Because the challenged work must be viewed as a whole,[7] it is doubtful that the Mapplethorpe exhibition could properly be regarded as either appealing to a prurient interest in sex or depicting sex in a patently offensive way. On these issues there might be some room for disagreement, but the situation is quite different when it comes to applying the third prong of the *Miller* test, which calls for an inquiry into the social value of the work and is meant to exclude from the ambit of constitutional protection the trivial or worthless, that is, material with no conceivable connection to the promotion of First Amendment values. Clearly, Mapplethorpe's work is not of that variety.

As a matter of aesthetics alone, the Mapplethorpe exhibition was a considerable achievement. His photographs were heartless; the flowers and bodies seemed devoid of life—as I said, they appeared almost sculptural—but they presented an aesthetic vision that was original and in many respects stunning. The fact that a number of the most respected museums in the country displayed the exhibition understandably made the work's aesthetic accomplishment the principal line of defense in the Cincinnati trial, and the testimony of leading figures from the national art establishment supported this aesthetic assessment. It is important, however, to understand that there was also a political dimension to Mapplethorpe's work, and it too called for protection under the *Miller* test, even more than did its aesthetic value.[8] The political significance of the exhibition derived from its revelatory power: It brought into view the lives and practices of the gay community, a group long marginalized in American society and today ravaged by the AIDS epidemic. The show was a response to the angry protest of the gay community: "Silence = Death."

The Mapplethorpe photographs bore witness to the life of the gay community, boldly affirming its understanding of the erotic, portraying the full range of the community's sexual practices, some intimate, some quite brutal. The intimate encounters—the kiss, for example—might be grudgingly accepted by the casual museum-goer, while the scenes characterized as sadomasochistic in the X, Y, Z Series forced the same viewer to confront, and thus critically to reflect upon, the limits of his or her tolerance.

Some of the shots in this series—for example, a picture of "a naked man with a bullwhip protruding from his posterior," as Senator Helms described it[9]—shocked conventional sensibilities in much the same way as burning a flag might. Like the confrontational tactics of gay political groups such as "ACT UP" and "Queer Nation," these photographs called on the viewer to recognize the gay community and its needs. This call was made all the more urgent by the AIDS crisis which, many charged, has been allowed to continue unabated because it afflicts a group whose suffering has often been dismissed by an unsympathetic public as insignificant or, worse, as deserved. One of the most striking photographs in the exhibition, perhaps emblematic of the entire show, was a 1988 self-portrait of Mapplethorpe, taken in the year before his death, in which only his face and his right hand are luminous, as though set in a sea of blackness. His face appears worn, his eyes distant and still, his right hand is clenched, grasping a staff crowned with a skull, which, like Mapplethorpe himself, stares out at the viewer.

Seen in this way, the Mapplethorpe exhibition was, to use the *Miller* test, endowed with serious political value. Indeed, I believe that on this basis alone the exhibition should have been protected from a criminal obscenity prosecution. But it is harder to evaluate the other type of state response occasioned by the show—a loss of federal subsidies. For most of our history, art in America has depended financially on the market and on private charity, but ever since the 1970s the federal government, through the National Endowment for the Arts, has played an increasingly important role in financially supporting or subsidizing artistic activity. The appropriation for the NEA for fiscal year 1990 was approximately $144 million.[10] The Institute of Contemporary Art of the University of Pennsylvania had received some $30,000 in NEA funds to assemble the Mapplethorpe retrospective. The question posed, in circumstances where the exhibition is protected from an obscenity prosecution, is whether it would have been constitutionally permissible for the government to deny that grant.

The controversy over funding the Mapplethorpe show began in June 1989 when Senator Helms learned that the show was about to open at the Corcoran Gallery of Art, a highly respected private museum in Washington, D.C. Senator Helms denounced Mapplethorpe's work as "filth" and "trash" and publicly objected to the use of federal funds to underwrite it.[11] The curator of the Corcoran Gallery, presumably acting out of fear for the impact of the controversy on the NEA or on future applications to the NEA by the Corcoran, responded by canceling the plans for the exhibition.

The Corcoran's decision to cancel the show angered the artistic community and, not surprisingly, did not satisfy or quiet the congressional critics. In the appropriations statute enacted that fall, Congress excluded from the NEA appropriations an amount equal to what the Institute of Contemporary Art had received for assembling the Mapplethorpe exhibition. The statute also required that the NEA give thirty days notice if it again intended to make a grant to the Institute.[12] The concern was not, however, only with the Mapplethorpe exhibition. Helms and his followers hoped to generalize these sanctions so that in the future the funds appropriated by Congress could not be used to support work like Mapplethorpe's.

Defining the category of artistic work that would be ineligible for NEA funds proved to be an arduous task, taxing the imagination of the lawyers and the negotiating skills of the politicians. The result was the so-called Helms amendment, which provided:

> None of the funds . . . may be used to promote, disseminate, or produce materials which in the judgment of the National Endowment for the Arts . . .

may be considered obscene, including but not limited to, depictions of sado-masochism, homoeroticism, the sexual exploitation of children, or individuals engaged in sex acts and which, when taken as a whole, do not have serious literary, artistic, political, or scientific value.[13]

Although the Helms amendment borrowed the language of the *Miller* test, the statute swept more broadly, prohibiting funding for projects that do not fall within *Miller*'s narrow definition of obscenity. Indeed, Senator Helms aspired to a rule prohibiting the government from funding all "indecent" art.[14]

The Helms amendment applied to funds appropriated by Congress in the summer of 1989, and, of necessity, expired when the period covered (fiscal year 1990) came to an end. However, the controversy stemming from the funding of the Mapplethorpe show persisted and took on additional significance in the summer of 1990, when Congress took up the question of reauthorizing the NEA and making appropriations for it. The result, a statute passed in November 1990, just after the jury verdict in Cincinnati and shortly before congressional elections, established a new statutory framework for the NEA, one that still controls to this day. The new statute avoided the language of the original Helms amendment yet nonetheless presents an equally serious, but perhaps less visible, threat to artistic freedom.

On one level, the 1990 statute appears to soften the censorial force of the Helms amendment. The statute still decrees that "obscenity . . . shall not be funded,"[15] but the determination of obscenity is left to the courts, and the standard articulated in the statute adopts the three-pronged *Miller* test. However, the new statute compounds the sanctions for an obscenity conviction by providing that if NEA funds are used to produce a work later decided by a court to be obscene, the funds will have to be repaid and the artist or recipient will be ineligible for further funding until full repayment is made.[16] This provision is a matter of some concern, since an increase in sanctions increases the deterrent effect of state obscenity laws, thereby enhancing the risk that someone might be discouraged from engaging in conduct that is constitutionally protected.

Even more worrisome are the provisions in the 1990 statute consolidating the power of the NEA chairperson over grantmaking. In the past, applications for grants were reviewed by panels of experts, usually peers of the applicant consisting of museum professionals or artists involved in the same discipline. These panels were deemed "advisory," but in practice they dominated the process—approval by a panel usually ensured receipt of a grant.[17] The 1990 revision sought to change that procedure, although the precise method by which that change will be effectuated is not specified.

The statute itself does no more than vest final authority for the selection of grantees in the chairperson.[18] Yet a commission was appointed by President Bush in the midst of the controversy engendered by the Helms amendment, and its report, issued in September 1990 in the midst of the congressional deliberations, should be read as part of the legislative history of the 1990 statute.[19] The report assumes that the chairperson will continue to use peer-review panels; but in order to concentrate responsibility for the selection in his or her hands, it recommends that the peer-review panels be asked to provide the chairperson with many more recommended applicants than can be funded. The chairperson will then choose the recipients.

What standards will be used in making this choice? On this issue the 1990 statute is explicit. It directs the chairperson to ensure that "artistic excellence and artistic merit are the criteria by which applications are judged, taking into consideration general standards of decency and respect for the diverse beliefs and values of the American public. . . . "[20] In directing the chairperson to attend to "general standards of decency," the 1990 statute, in effect, transforms the Helms amendment into an internal operating principle of the NEA. The chairperson is freed from the *Miller* standards and is able to deny funding to a project like Mapplethorpe's even though it is not within the constitutional definition of obscenity and thus not lawfully subject to criminal prosecution. The chairperson could conclude that the project offends "general standards of decency," even though it has, within the meaning of the Supreme Court's standards, serious aesthetic or political value. If he or she does, Senator Helms will have had his way.[21]

II

Most commentators and perhaps a majority of the Supreme Court would not see this decency standard in the 1990 statute as posing a First Amendment problem of any sort, but my inclination is just the opposite. I begin with the assumption that government subsidies are not gifts or bonuses for acts that would have occurred without them. Subsidies are not redundant, but rather have a productive value: NEA grants bring into existence art, performances, or exhibitions that would not otherwise exist. They do this either by providing artists with an income, by defraying costs associated with a show, or by creating incentives for artists or the distributors of art. The grant to the Institute for Contemporary Art for the Mapplethorpe exhibition, for example, encouraged, or made possible the Mapplethorpe exhibition; the denial of that subsidy would have had the effect of withdrawing the exhibition from public view or limiting its availability. A denial of a grant does not have the brutal consequences for the individual that might, on the worst of days, attend a criminal prosecution for obscenity, when the artist languishes in prison. From the perspective of the public, however, its effect is similar: It keeps art from us.

Of course, even without the government grant, the artistic endeavor may survive and be made available to the public. Alternative sources of funds might be found, as might have occurred in the case of the Mapplethorpe show itself if the original grant had been denied the Institute of Contemporary Art. In that sense, the ban effectuated by a denial of grants, even federal ones, is not absolute and universal. To borrow a term from Harry Kalven, it is a "partial sanction."[22] I believe the same might well be said of the criminal prosecution. An artist or museum director might decide to suffer the sanction of the criminal law (for example, pay the fine or spend some time in jail) rather than remain silent. Or, as became evident in the case of Mapplethorpe, the criminal sanction might be limited in its geographic reach because the administration of the criminal law is largely the responsibility of states and localities, which have limited jurisdictions. The Mapplethorpe exhibition provoked an obscenity prosecution in Cincinnati, but not in Philadelphia or Hartford (where it was shown previously) or in Boston (where it moved subsequently).

It is thus appropriate to assume that the effect on the public of a denial of a grant is roughly equivalent to that of a criminal prosecution, in that each tends to silence the artist or, in the case of exhibitions, makes the artist's work unavailable to the general museum-going public. But a complication is introduced when it comes time to define the constitutional wrong. In the criminal context, the wrong can be defined in purely quantitative terms, that is, in terms of the overall quantity or amount of speech available to the public. Indeed, our reaction to the obscenity prosecution is largely shaped by the common assumption that the more speech the better; the function of the three-pronged definition of obscenity is to keep that silencing effect to an absolute minimum. In the case of subsidies, however, an additional element is needed to define the wrong, because the presence of scarcity transforms the decisional process into an allocative one.

The amount of money to be dispensed by government will always be exceeded by the number of applicants, and thus a competition will arise among the applicants for the grants. A grant given to one is necessarily de-nied to another. A grant for the Mapplethorpe exhibition enhanced the availability of his work to the public, but that money was denied to an-other artist, thereby limiting the availability of that artist's work and in that sense silencing him or her. Conversely, while denying a grant for the Mapplethorpe show might have limited the availability of his work to the public, one can also assume that the funds withheld would not have lain idle but would have been allocated to some other artist, allowing that artist's work to flourish. This means that the silencing produced by the de-nial of the subsidy is of a different nature than that produced by a crimi-nal prosecution. The difference arises from the fact that silencing is a nec-essary concomitant of every allocative decision.[23]

At this point, the temptation is great to retreat from the concern with ef-fect and, in contrast to the criminal context, to define the constitutional wrong in purely procedural terms. While the wrong in the criminal con-text consists of the silencing effect, which the constitutional definition of obscenity tries to keep to a minimum, the wrong in the allocative context is not the silencing effect but rather the reason or criterion upon which the allocation in question was based. Under this view, the First Amendment would be reduced to a rule requiring that the choice among applicants not be made on the basis of a forbidden criterion.

To support this view, an analogy might be drawn to the body of consti-tutional doctrine concerning the treatment of women and racial minorities under conditions of scarcity in, say, employment. In that context, the Court has abandoned the approach it had taken in the late 1960s and early 1970s, and beginning with *Washington v. Davis* in 1976, has taken the po-sition that the constitutional wrong consists not of the effect (denial of em-ployment) but the use of a forbidden criterion (race or sex).[24] I have great difficulty with this shift in the Court's approach to equal protection or dis-crimination issues, and am even more troubled by the notion of transfer-ring it to free speech.

While in the discrimination context it might be possible to construct a fi-nite and rather well-understood list of forbidden criteria (race, religion, na-tional origin, sex, etc.), in the free speech context no such list readily sug-gests itself. What are the criteria prohibited by the First Amendment? In a library case, Justice Brennan grappled with a similar problem and, in an effort to honor the general norm of content neutrality, used two notions to define the forbidden criterion: disagreement with an idea and a desire to suppress that idea. He said that a library's decision to remove a book from its collection cannot be based on a disagreement with the ideas presented in that book and a desire to limit access to those ideas.[25] But, as with any allocative decision, the acquisition and removal decisions of a library must reflect some judgment as to what ideas to make available to readers and what not to make available. It is not at all clear why the First Amendment would prohibit that judgment from being based on agreement or disagreement with those ideas, or any other reaction to the content of the material. In the allocative context, content neutrality makes little sense, for a choice must be made among competing ideas, and for that purpose the official entrusted with that decision must look to content. Surely, books should be purchased, or artistic awards granted, on the basis of content.

Moreover, even if the forbidden criteria could be identified with some specificity, a First Amendment approach that looked to the criteria used in an allocation would be extremely difficult to administer. This is especially true for awards made under the 1990 NEA statute. Such an approach entails an inquiry into the grounds or basis of a decision, and, as we know from the discrimination context, often the real reason for an allocative decision cannot be authoritatively ascertained. Imagine that a peer-review panel provides the NEA chairperson with a list of a dozen applicants under circumstances where only one can be funded. The chairperson chooses the one, and then justifies his or her decision on grounds of "artistic excellence." How can a court be certain that this is the real reason for the chairperson's decision and that the chairperson is not basing it on some (still to be defined) forbidden criterion or, to use a phrase of Brennan's from the library case, that he or she is not impelled by an "unconstitutional motivation"? Granted, the legal system might cope with this problem by creating presumptions or devising various rules regarding the burden of proof, but all these devices will invariably reflect some understanding of effect or impact. Similarly, the legal system will have to fall back on notions of effect, as it has done in the discrimination context after *Washington v. Davis,* to deal with the problems of multimember decisional agencies (one official bases his or her decision on the forbidden criterion while the others do not) or mixed motives (the allocative decision is only partially based on the forbidden criterion).

It is also hard to understand the theoretical basis of an approach looking to the decisional criteria. In the discrimination context, the criterion approach rests upon considerations of individual fairness—it is arbitrary to judge someone on the basis of a criterion (such as race or gender) that has no discernible connection to productivity and over which the individual has no control. I, for one, believe it is a mistake to reduce the constitutional ideal of equality to considerations of individual unfairness,[26] but however appropriate such a reduction might be in the discrimination context, it seems particularly inappropriate in the speech context. The First Amendment is a guarantee of collective self-determination, a method for making certain that the people know all that they must to exercise their sovereign prerogative, and for that reason, the focus should be on the condition of public discourse, not the process by which that condition was created.[27] Keeping ideas and information from the public, not the unfair treatment of the speaker, is the gist of the constitutional wrong, and as a consequence, a concern with the basis or criteria for the act that keeps ideas from the public makes little theoretical sense. As Justice Rehnquist put it in the library case, though only to score a debater's point, "If Justice Brennan truly recognizes a constitutional right to receive information, it is difficult to see why the reason for the denial makes any difference."[28]

In the discrimination context, some have defended the criterion approach on the ground that it maintains a measure of state neutrality: If a judgment is based on some meritocratic criterion, such as performance on standardized tests, the state can achieve a measure of neutrality on issues of race even though it must make a choice among applicants for a job. A similar thought might account for the use of the criterion approach in the religion context in order to maintain the separation of church and state. It might also have some sway in the speech area, where we want the state to be neutral between competing viewpoints, and where it might be assumed that neutrality could be achieved by having allocative decisions based on some meritocratic criterion such as "artistic excellence."

This assumption, however, is unfounded. The ideal of neutrality in the speech context not only requires that the state refrain from choosing among viewpoints, but also that it not structure public discourse in such a way as to favor one viewpoint over another. The state must act as a high-minded parliamentarian, making certain that all viewpoints are fully and fairly heard. In the allocative context, the state's decision will necessarily have an impact on which viewpoints are heard by the public, and the state's obligation of neutrality requires that it make certain that the public debate is as rich and varied as possible. The use of a meritocratic criterion cannot ensure the discharge of this duty, for it disregards the impact of that decision on public debate.

We learned in the discrimination context that a seemingly neutral criterion does not ensure a neutral impact. A meritocratic criterion, such as a standardized test, may still have a discriminatory effect, because it may especially disadvantage minorities. Similarly, in the speech context, the use of a meritocratic criterion, such as "artistic excellence," for determining who is heard may silence viewpoints or skew debate. Of course, whether this occurs will depend on the specific content given the (rather broad-ranging) notion of "artistic excellence" and on the condition and needs of public discourse.

For these reasons, the judiciary should not adopt a criterion approach in judging allocations or other affirmative exercises of state power. Rather, it should keep the focus on effects, specifically the effect that the exercise of state power has on public debate. In a case like Mapplethorpe's, the denial of a grant would impoverish public debate because it would reinforce the prevailing orthodoxy on an issue of great public importance, the status of the gay community, and the basis for that denial, whether it be aesthetics, taste, or ideology, is of no constitutional significance. The constitutional wrong of an obscenity prosecution arises from the effect such an exercise of state power has upon public discourse, and although there is an analytic difference in the subsidy situation, arising from the scarcity factor, the focus should remain on the effect of the government action. The difference between the two situations requires not an abandonment of the concern with effect, but a more refined conception of effect and the introduction of a more qualitative perspective in the allocative context: A court must determine what effect a challenged allocative decision would have upon public debate. To use the now talismanic phrase, a court must ascertain whether the allocative decision would contribute to a debate on national issues that is "uninhibited, robust, and wide-open,"[29] or whether its effect would be just the opposite.

III

An approach to allocative decisions that looks to effect has its own difficulties. For one thing, it requires a sense of the public agenda, a grasp of the issues that are now before the public and that might plausibly be brought before it. It also requires an appraisal of the state of public discourse, not to decide who is right or wrong, but to see whether all the positions on an issue are being fully and fairly presented so that the people can make a meaningful choice. These kinds of judgments must be context-specific, and perhaps for that very reason they seem extremely arduous. They are, however, required by the grandest aspirations of the Constitution, and they are not beyond our reach. In fact, they are analogous to the judgments made by the great teachers of the universities of this nation every day of the week as they structure discussion in their classes. Judgments such as these are even implicit in our assessment of the Mapplethorpe controversy: The special egregiousness of the denial of NEA funding in such a case arises from the fact that it would perpetuate and reinforce the orthodoxy that tends to marginalize the gay community. Even those on the side of censorship in this controversy would acknowledge this effect; in fact, they may wish it to occur.

The judgments required by the effects approach have analogues throughout the law, not just in discrimination cases, but also in such disparate areas as antitrust, when a judge determines the parameters of a relevant market, and torts, when a judge evaluates the frontiers of scientific possibility in order to adjudicate a state-of-the-art defense. Admittedly, we may be especially reluctant to allow these judgments in the speech area because we fear that the judicial power will become an instrument for constricting rather than broadening public understanding or, even worse, for favoring one viewpoint over another. In assessing the significance of this risk, however, two considerations must be kept in mind.

First, the courts will not make these judgments in a vacuum, but will be subject to intense scrutiny from the critical community that attends to matters judicial—in this instance, not just lawyers and the press, but also the leaders of the art world. The Mapplethorpe controversy was remarkable in its capacity to mobilize the art community and to spur countless museums and theaters across the country into action. If judicial review of a funding decision were required, members of this community might participate in the judicial proceedings, as they did in the Cincinnati trial, to help the court appreciate the political and aesthetic significance of the work denied funding. Or, they might mobilize the public, as they did in response to the Helms amendment, to make certain that the judiciary does not shirk its duty, or become an instrument of censorship, while reviewing NEA practices under the effects standard. The courts may be less responsive to such criticism than institutions that are politically accountable, but they are not immune to it.

Second, a rejection of the effects approach, and a willingness to judge allocations on the basis of decisional criteria, would invite the very same risk—namely, that courts will become an instrument for perpetuating an orthodoxy—but it would do so in an even more flagrant manner. The ev-

identiary difficulties of sorting out the real reason for a decision and im-
peaching the stated reason will tilt the process in favor of the NEA, and
almost invariably lead to the endorsement of its decisions.

Even under the effects approach, state officials are likely to continue
using meritocratic criteria, such as "artistic excellence," to allocate grants.
The NEA will select what it understands to be the best or most worthy recipient. The agency will, however, come to understand that its standards
of excellence will have to be either interpreted, or modified, in light of the
constitutional commitment to robust public debate. When a criterion such
as "artistic excellence" is used in such a way as to have the consequence
of keeping from public view art that presents ideas and positions otherwise absent from public discourse, and thus constrains public debate, it
will have to be qualified in order to remain consistent with the purposes
of the First Amendment.[30]

Considerations of merit will also have a role to play when it comes time
for the judiciary to review a denial of a grant. As in the early discrimination cases, where the Supreme Court looked to effects,[31] judgments of
artistic merit emerge as a justification or defense for a course of conduct
that produces the undesirable effect (the perpetuation of an orthodoxy). As
a defense, considerations of artistic merit fix the outer limits on the state's
duty to avoid the production of that effect, and the precise location of that
limitation depends on the gravity of the effect produced and the urgency
of the justification for what the state has done. The duty to attend to effects in the speech area does not mean, any more than it did in the area of
race, an end to merit. What it does mean is either a reexamination of the
notions of merit that underlie funding decisions or, alas, a sacrifice of
some of the values furthered by notions of merit that do not incorporate,
or, in fact, are antagonistic to, the constitutional goal of producing a public debate that is worthy of our democratic aspirations.

In determining whether there would in fact be such a sacrifice, and what
its magnitude might be, it is important to understand how art typically per-
forms its educative function: not by advancing a single viewpoint, in the
way that a commercial advertisement or political propaganda might, but
by leading the viewer to contemplate a familiar subject from a new perspective or by bringing the unfamiliar into focus. The best art leads us to
ponder, reconsider, suspend conventional wisdom, and reject unreflective
assumptions and expectations. Subjectively, art provokes an attitude of inquisitiveness; objectively, it reveals aspects of an experience or subject
matter—in the case of Mapplethorpe, sexuality—that we have previously
misperceived or ignored. The best art is art that enriches public discourse,

not in the manner Stalin made familiar, but by opening our eyes and thereby transforming our understanding of the world.

The Mapplethorpe exhibition was not by any means a simple and straightforward celebration of homosexuality or gay life, nor was that the basis for its special claim for public support. The Mapplethorpe exhibition brought the gay community into focus, but only to complicate our understanding of it. Certainly, the photographs were defiant affirmations of gay sexuality, but they were also something more. Their manner of presenting their subject through classically simple composition and immaculately clear, precise renderings of sensuous surfaces, recalling fashion photography, had the effect of making the activities depicted appear staged or theatrical, as if the participants were merely performing for others, or as if their self-awareness depended on how they appeared in others' eyes. These images suggest a parallel between, on the one hand, a theatrical sexuality that may have as much to do with posing, and even pain, as with emotion,[32] and, on the other hand, the social position of gay people in contemporary America, simultaneously marginalized and subjected to intense and derisive public scrutiny. Walking through the exhibit, one was led to wonder whether social marginalization had been internalized in homosexual practice—whether homosexual self-understanding had been marred and distorted by public loathing and opprobrium. Mapplethorpe's photographs did not constitute a propagandistic endorsement of homosexuality, or anything else, but invited us—all of us—to reconsider our understanding of, and attitude toward, homosexual orientation and practice. There was no sacrifice of either artistic or democratic values. Mapplethorpe's photographs were, at once, great art and a great lecture, an inspired contribution to a public debate that promises to be "uninhibited, robust, and wide-open."

There is, of course, a danger that the government might respond to judicial review of decisions denying grants to such controversial and provocative works by withdrawing from the field altogether. The state might abandon the subsidy program, or at least seriously cut back on it, in which case speech would be a loser to an even greater extent than when the government denies a grant to some controversial artist. The Mapplethorpe controversy did indeed result in diminution of the NEA appropriation in the 1989 funding statute and provoked a call—that continues to this day—for an end to government funding for the arts.[33] In the criminal context, there is no comparable risk because a state retreat—no prosecution or repeal of an obscenity statute—is assumed under standard doctrine to promote speech values.

It seems to me, however, that this difference between the criminal and allocative contexts requires a measure of caution, not a difference in standards or general approach. The reduction of the overall level of arts funding is a contingency, not a necessity. The judiciary should not assume that it will materialize and, in fact, should do all that it can to prevent that from happening, always keeping open the possibility that, in the worst of all possible worlds, it might have to mandate a freeze or even an increase in levels of spending to protect First Amendment values. The Constitution commands that Congress make no law abridging the freedom of speech, but as in the case of the heckler's veto, where a speaker is left to the mercy of an angry mob, a decision of the state not to act—to go out of the funding business altogether—might itself be a form of action prohibited by the First Amendment.[34] The broad discretion allowed the legislature in making budgetary decisions cannot be used in a way that interferes with the attainment of constitutional goals or, more concretely, with the judiciary's efforts to further these goals by reviewing the programs established by the legislature and the way they have been administered by the executive.

In the school desegregation area, strong judicial intervention created a risk that the school boards would close their schools rather than integrate. It is remarkable, however, that over a thirty-year period, involving thousands and thousands of court desegregation orders, that risk materialized only on two or three occasions, and in each instance, the judiciary somehow found that it had the power to order that the schools be reopened.[35] This power was not defeated by sloganistic assertions that "there is no constitutional right to a public education" (which have recurred in the art context in slightly different form);[36] indeed, this judicial power was affirmed in 1990 by the Supreme Court in the Kansas City school case, in which a federal court ordered the state to raise taxes to finance the court's desegregation plan.[37]

As a purely ideological matter, the argument in favor of a double standard, sharply differentiating between subsidies and criminal prosecutions, and applying a distinctly more relaxed standard to the former, has many roots; but perhaps none is more important today than the capitalist ethos that transforms money into power and gives to each productive agent prerogatives over the property or money he or she has earned. Capitalism contemplates private ownership of the means of production and, even more crucially, a sharply differentiated incentive structure. The best get paid the most. For this incentive structure to work as promised, the rewards distributed for efficient production must be secured from the "rapacious greed" of the less well paid and, even more, must empower those who are fortunate enough to receive these rewards. The private property system presupposed by capitalism is intended to provide to each individual, with respect to the money he or she has earned, a sense of entitlement as well as a sense of security. You may use your money in the way you wish, spend it on the goods you want, give it to anyone you wish, or deny it to those you do not like or admire.

There is no reason in the world why the sense of entitlement associated with private property should extend to the money in the public treasury, which is not earned but rather collected and held for public purposes. But in this triumphant moment of capitalism, the norms of this economic system cannot easily be confined. Money is money, and what is worse, we tend to think of the state in much the same way as we would an individual entrepreneur, confusing Uncle Sam and Donald Trump. We personify the state and accord it the privileges of a productive agent, thinking that the decision of the government to support activities should be wholly discretionary and that government should not be obliged to support activities it does not like or admire.[38]

What is needed here by way of remedy is a sense of limits. One can readily appreciate the marvels of capitalism as an economic system, as a way of providing for the efficient delivery of goods and services, without believing that each and every decision of social life—say, of the political domain or of the family—should be dominated by the norms of that economic system. It would be sad if the First Amendment became captured by capitalism and if we thus allowed free speech to be compromised by our desire to protect private property. The revenues collected by the state constitute a public resource, to be used for public purposes, and I can think of no higher purpose for these funds than the preservation of democracy, bringing before the public viewpoints and options that otherwise might be slighted or ignored. Government subsidies, whether they be for the arts or education, should not be used to reinforce prevailing orthodoxies, but rather to further the sovereignty of the people by provoking and stirring public debate, so that we may live as we do because we want to, not because the familiar is all we know or can imagine.

6

The Right Kind
of Neutrality

PROLOGUE

In my article State Activism and State Censorship *(Chapter 5), I had to cope with an objection raised by a number of liberal theorists about the requirement of state neutrality. For them, the state could satisfy that requirement only by getting out of the business of subsidizing speech activities altogether. Such a withdrawal did not seem to me very neutral, for it would leave speech in the grips of the market. After long discussions with one of my assistants, Jennifer Brown, I introduced the notion of the state as a parliamentarian to explain how the state might make choices among speakers and still be neutral.*

In the essay that follows—delivered as lectures in February 1995 at Capital University Law School and Tulane and published, along with spirited replies, in the fall of 1995 in the Capital University Law Review—*I further explore the notion of the state as parliamentarian. The immediate context is hate speech—a problem that has received increasing attention in recent years and that, like the problem of pornography, raises important issues about social inequalities and their significance for free speech doctrine.*

In depicting the state as a parliamentarian, I seemed to have backed into an idea that was sporadically used by Harry Kalven and, before him, Alexander Meiklejohn. Recently, that idea was forcefully criticized by Robert Post—alas, another favorite student. His article, Meiklejohn's Mistake: On Individual Autonomy and the Reform of Public Discourse, *first appeared in 1993 in the* University of Colorado Law Review *and has been reprinted in his* Constitutional Domains: Democracy, Community, Management *(1995). In this essay, I try to respond to Post's article, and I make reference to a more extended response by Morris Lipson in 1995 in a Note in the* Yale Law Journal.

Imagine a community that traditionally has been all white. A black family moves into the community. They purchase a house. Some neighbors are upset about the arrival of this new family. At first, these particular neighbors are content to show their displeasure by snubbing the new arrivals, but soon the situation changes for the worse. One night, someone places a cross on public property in front of the black family's home and sets the cross afire.

Afterward, the perpetrators are apprehended and prosecuted. They are charged with violating a local statute that prohibits expressive activities (including cross-burning) that cause anger, alarm, or resentment in individuals who are singled out on the basis of their race, religion, or gender. The perpetrators defend themselves on the ground that the statute violates their First Amendment rights.

In 1992, in *R.A.V. v. City of St. Paul*, the Supreme Court considered an analogous case and, in an opinion written by Justice Scalia, declared the challenged statute unconstitutional.[1] That ruling, one of the most important pronouncements of the Rehnquist Court on free speech, caused an enormous stir within constitutional circles and divided many of those who have long viewed themselves as friends of the First Amendment. The Court used the occasion to proclaim the priority of free speech over other constitutional values, even equality, and gave a ringing endorsement to the rule requiring content neutrality. But the Court overlooked the fact that it was confronted with one of those situations—explored throughout this book—where the state might have to curtail the speech of some to let the less powerful be heard.

I

Initially it should be stressed that the *R.A.V.* Court did not focus on the act of cross-burning. Justice Scalia did not suggest that cross-burning itself is constitutionally protected or immune from state regulation. Rather, the Court objected to the specific statute under which the individuals were prosecuted. The Court held the statute unconstitutional on its face and ruled that it could not be applied to anyone, whether accused of burning a cross or of engaging in any of the other prohibited activities.

In its entirety, the St. Paul ordinance provided: "Whoever places on public or private property a symbol, object, appellation, characterization or graffiti, including, but not limited to, a burning cross or Nazi swastika, which one knows or has reasonable grounds to know arouses anger, alarm or resentment in others on the basis of race, color, creed, religion or gender commits disorderly conduct and shall be guilty of a misdemeanor."[2]

In enacting this measure, the city was trying to regulate the kinds of symbols that could be placed on public or private property; by way of enumeration, the ordinance mentioned one of the most notorious racist symbols in America—a burning cross, a symbol long associated with the Ku Klux Klan, typically used to convey the view that blacks are not welcome in the community. Clearly, the St. Paul ordinance could be characterized as a regulation of expression.

In judging the validity of this law, Scalia wisely avoided an approach— once heralded by Justice Black—that would have condemned the ordinance simply because it was a regulation of expression or speech. The First Amendment provides, "Congress shall make no law abridging the freedom of speech," and, laying the foundation for a certain kind of absolutism, Justice Black insisted again and again that "no law" means "no law."[3]

Once a loyal New Deal Democrat in the Senate, Black was placed on the Court by President Roosevelt during the 1930s and was, from the very beginning, determined to avoid the pitfalls of *Lochner v. New York*[4] and other decisions of the Supreme Court that wreaked havoc on the New Deal. At the core of Black's judicial philosophy was an aversion to "substantive due process" and the kind of discretion that it provided to judges to strike down laws they found "arbitrary" or "unreasonable."[5] As a result, the Justice rejected any constitutional interpretation that would force the Court to make such open-ended judgments. He sought refuge in literalism, looking for the plain and simple meaning of constitutional provisions, and in the domain of free speech, this aspiration led to an absolutism.

Many justices have sympathized with Black's general quest, and I would include Scalia among them, but the fact remains that Black's First Amendment absolutism never received the support of a majority of the Court. Indeed, over the years, it picked up only one vote—that of Justice William Douglas. It was obvious that Black's literalism was selective, for he read the word "Congress" to include both the Executive and the Judiciary. A selective literalism must presuppose some theory to explain which phrases should be given their ordinary meaning and which ones not, and thus cannot be a form of pure literalism. Moreover, the kind of judgments Black so feared would necessarily have to be made in determining whether some forms of human behavior constituted "speech" rather than "action." Surely, he would want the First Amendment to protect, as the Court indeed has held, not just verbal utterances—"speech" as it is ordinarily or literally understood—but also films, novels, parading, and even burning a flag.

Justice Black made a great deal out of the phrase "no law," but was less careful about identifying the laws that the First Amendment actually prohibited. This was no trivial oversight. As Alexander Meiklejohn emphasized, what the First Amendment prohibits is law that abridges "the freedom of speech," not the freedom *to* speak.[6] The phrase "the freedom of speech" implies an organized and structured understanding of freedom, one that recognizes that the state's power over speech is limited but not denied altogether. In contrast to Black's view, the approach of the Court— in *R.A.V.* and elsewhere—has been to permit regulations of speech, but to confine them to the smallest domain necessary to enable the state to conduct its other vital functions.

By its very terms, the St. Paul ordinance seemed to reach very broadly, perhaps too broadly. The Supreme Court of Minnesota was aware of its sweep and, in an effort to bring the ordinance within the scope of regulation traditionally allowed, construed the ordinance to be confined to "fighting words." This phrase refers to a category of expression that is likely to provoke an immediate violent reaction by the persons to whom the words are addressed and that also conveys little by way of ideas and thus makes only the most limited contribution to public debate. For these reasons, in one of its early free speech decisions, the Supreme Court of the United States held that "fighting words" are unprotected or, to put it another way, within the power of the state to suppress.[7]

This interpretation of the St. Paul ordinance narrows its scope, but does not eliminate the First Amendment problem altogether, for as Justice Scalia stressed in *R.A.V.*, "fighting words" are still words. "Fighting words" may be subject to state regulation, but because they are sometimes a means for conveying an opinion or advancing a position and thus part of the rough-and-tumble of public discourse, one must be sensitive to the *way* they are regulated.

What Scalia found objectionable with the way St. Paul proceeded in this regulation of speech arose from the partiality of the law. This may seem puzzling since in one sense the St. Paul ordinance was comprehensive. It covered the expressive activities of racists of all persuasions that might arouse alarm or anger in their targets, whether those activities were aimed at whites or blacks. On the other hand, the statute did not cover the activities of those fighting racism—the anti-racists. Obviously, those fighting racism are not about to burn crosses to promote their ideas, but they have their own symbols or appellations that may cause anger, alarm, or resentment in others—their own "fighting words." For example, they might place graffiti on public property accusing their opponents of being Nazis or they might burn the American flag in front of the houses of those whom they believe harbor racist views. The St. Paul ordinance did not, by its very terms, cover those activities, and from this limitation on its coverage, Justice Scalia concluded that the law discriminated on the basis of viewpoint and thus ran afoul of one of the governing principles of the First Amendment. In what I take to be the crucial passage in his analysis, Scalia declared: "St. Paul has no . . . authority to license one side of a debate to fight freestyle, while requiring the other to follow Marquis of Queensbury Rules."[8]

Underlying the principle banning viewpoint discrimination is an understanding of the First Amendment, central to this book and now almost axiomatic in the profession, that treats that law as an instrument of democratic self-government. According to this view, the purpose of the First Amendment is to protect the sovereignty of the people to decide how they wish to live their lives. The state is not to make that choice for the people, and, even more relevantly for our purposes, the state is not allowed to manipulate public debate in a way that effectively determines that choice. The state must remain neutral between competing viewpoints. In Justice Scalia's eyes, St. Paul breached this obligation to remain neutral when it enacted a measure limiting the expressive activities of racists, but not of those fighting racism.

II

Many who have criticized the *R.A.V.* decision acknowledge the nonneutrality of the St. Paul ordinance, but justify this differential treatment in terms of the substantive value underlying the state's intervention: equality.[9] It is perfectly permissible, these critics say, for the city to favor the antiracists because the Thirteenth, Fourteenth, and Fifteenth Amendments, as well as all the statutes enacted to enforce those provisions, condemn racism. Those fighting racism could be viewed as furthering the egalitarian goals of the Constitution—they are the soldiers of the Constitution—and should be allowed certain advantages in public debate over the proponents of racism. True, the city is not being neutral, but since it is favoring a position that is itself favored by the Constitution, there is no reason for concern.

This critique of *R.A.V.* raises far-reaching questions about the limits of self-governance. Should an individual be able to urge action inconsistent with one of the organizing principles of our constitutional order, and should the First Amendment protect his or her right to do so? There is a tradition in the First Amendment, perhaps best illustrated in the modern period by the hostile reaction of most liberals to the anti-Communist crusade of the 1950s, that conceives of the right of self-governance in the broadest terms and answers this question in the affirmative. Everything is up for grabs, even fundamental principles. It is almost as though the First Amendment gives rise to a right of revolution.

The Communists were charged with advocating the violent overthrow of government—a repudiation of the Constitution in its entirety—and liberal critics of McCarthyism argued that this option should be presented to the people, if only so it could be subject to scrutiny and duly rejected. In the end, the Court embraced the liberal position,[10] and those decisions might be marshaled to support *R.A.V.* On Scalia's behalf, some might well insist that the First Amendment protects the advocacy of racism or, even further, the repudiation of the Civil War amendments and all the statutes enacted under them. No matter what the issue, the state must not take sides or, more to the point, tilt the debate one way or the other.

Over the years, the Supreme Court has struck a delicate balance between preserving the state's neutrality in public debate and enabling the state to exercise its police power. As a result, even at its most liberal moments, the Supreme Court has been measured in its protection of subversive advocacy. Communists were allowed to engage in the general advocacy of revolution, but the Court drew the line when advocacy turned into incitement. Similarly, it could be argued that although racists should be able to advocate on behalf of inequality—they can write a book urging repeal of the Civil War amendments or hold a rally on the green proclaiming theories of racial superiority—they should not be entitled to express their views by burning a cross in front of a black family's house at night. Such an expressive activity might be considered a "threat" or "harassment" and treated as comparable to an "incitement"—a speech act that is temporally proximate to a harm that the state has an unquestioned right to restrict. To deny the state the power to interfere with such a speech act is to deny it the power to prevent the harm.

All of this is true, yet it is worth emphasizing again that the Court in *R.A.V.* was making a judgment about the ordinance, not the activity; it may well be that the state has to have the power to suppress cross-burning as part of a comprehensive regulation of threats, harassment, or "fighting words." Nothing in *R.A.V.* precluded that possibility. What the decision turned on was the fact that the St. Paul ordinance was a partial regulation of speech: It covered the "fighting words" of racists, but not comparable expressions of those opposed to racism. It would be as though the state sought to regulate the incitements of Communists but not capitalists.

The liberal position on the Communist cases, and Scalia's objection to the partiality of the St. Paul ordinance, are premised on a view that accords a very privileged position to free speech. In effect, Scalia is saying that debate on all public issues must be uninhibited and wide open, even when it puts a constitutional value such as equality in jeopardy. The First Amendment is first.[11] The critics of the *R.A.V.* decision have insisted that such an ordering of constitutional values remains unjustified—in the conflict between liberty and equality, it is not clear why liberty should prevail. Such an ordering of values may well be consistent with classical liberal philosophy, with its exclusive devotion to individual liberty, but contemporary liberalism, especially as forged by the civil rights struggles of the 1960s, is defined by a dual commitment—to liberty and to equality.

The major premise of *R.A.V.* is vulnerable on this score. Yet those who criticize *R.A.V.* on this ground are no more secure in their premises than Scalia—in the conflict between liberty and equality, they assert the priority of equality without much more by way of justification. The upshot is an impasse, where liberals are divided among themselves. One group asserts the priority of liberty and the other the priority of equality, and neither provides any principled basis for deciding between them. Liberals are being asked to choose between their defining values.

III

In reflecting on the dilemma now confronting liberals, it occurs to me that it might be possible, at least for purposes of argument, to allow Justice Scalia his major premise—assume the firstness of the First Amendment— and still find the partiality of the St. Paul regulation acceptable. As with the arguments I advance in the context of pornography (Chapter 4) and campaign finance (Chapter 1), this approach looks to the silencing effects of speech. It is premised on the view that cross-burning not only insults blacks and interferes with their right to choose where they wish to live, but also interferes with their speech rights. It discourages them from participating in the deliberative activities of society. They feel less entitled and less inclined to voice their views in the public square, and withdraw unto themselves. They are silenced almost as effectively as if the state intervened to silence them.

Seen from this perspective, St. Paul's intervention might be analogized to that of a parliamentarian trying to protect the integrity of public debate. The city is trying to ensure that the speech rights of black citizens are protected; the ordinance is partial because the city has made the judgment that racists do not require such protection, and indeed that certain of their speech activities—for example, burning a cross, but perhaps not publishing a book or walking down Main Street in white hoods or Nazi uniforms—have to be curbed in order to protect the expressive activities of blacks in the community. St. Paul is silencing some to allow others to speak.

In intervening in this manner, the city is protecting the speech rights of the blacks, and it assumes that it can do so only by restricting the range of speech acts available to racists. In favoring the speech rights of blacks in this way, the municipality is not making a judgment about the merit—constitutional or otherwise—of the views each side is likely to express. Rather, it is declaring that this sector of the community must be heard from more fully if the public is to make an informed choice about an entire range of issues on the public agenda, from affirmative action, to education, to welfare policy. The city is acting as a parliamentarian trying to end a pattern of behavior that tends to silence one group and thus distorts or skews public debate. It is not trying to usurp the public's right of collective self-determination, but rather to enhance the public's capacity to properly exercise that right.

Admittedly, such intervention is likely to have an effect on the choices of the people. Every regulation of process affects outcome. But this impact on outcome is comparable to the effect on outcome that arises when a parliamentarian insists that all sides be heard. While participants in a meeting may vote differently when they hear all sides of the debate rather than one, this is something to applaud, rather than condemn. The principle of democratic self-governance enshrined by the First Amendment does not simply protect choice by citizens, but rather a choice made with adequate information and under suitable conditions of reflection.

In an earlier period, First Amendment theorists such as Alexander Meiklejohn and Harry Kalven—the architects of the liberal position on free speech—often used the metaphor of the parliamentarian to define an appropriate role for state regulation of speech.[12] They conceived of society as one gigantic town meeting and, within this framework, defended "time, place, and manner" regulations and explained why the "heckler's veto" was so objectionable. Recently, Professor Robert Post has criticized this use of the notion of a "town meeting" and the conclusion that the state could be viewed as a parliamentarian. He has insisted that such a view ultimately rests on antidemocratic assumptions.[13]

According to Post, while actual town meetings take place against a background in which the participants agree to an agenda—sometimes implicitly or informally—no such assumptions can be made about civil society. In civil society, no one is ever out of order. Civil society, he argued, can be thought of as a town meeting only if it too has an agenda, but that would require a certain measure of dictatorial action by the state and a disregard of democratic principles, which require that citizens set the public agenda and always be free to reset it.

The notion of a town meeting does indeed presuppose an agenda—there must be some standard of relevance—but agendas, either of actual town meetings or of the more metaphoric type, need not be set by the deliberate action of the participants nor imposed by an external force, such as the state. They can evolve more organically. In democratic societies, there is always an agenda that structures public discussion—one week nuclear proliferation, the next health care—even though that agenda is not set by anyone in particular.

Of course, the role I envision for the state as parliamentarian is more ambitious than that contemplated by Kalven and Meiklejohn. For the most part, they assumed that the state could discharge its duty as a parliamentarian simply by following something akin to Robert's Rules of Order: a predetermined method of proceeding that does not turn on the substance of what is transpiring or what is being said in the debate, but rather on some universal procedural principle like temporal priority. Indeed, it was Kalven, writing in the early 1970s, who did so much to place the rule against content regulation—the rule invoked by Justice Scalia—at the foundation of the First Amendment tradition.[14] I doubt Kalven would have reified it in the way the Court has since he wrote, but in any event it seems clear today that the state should not be confined to Robert's Rules of Order when acting as a parliamentarian. A fair-minded parliamentarian must be sensitive to the excesses of advocacy and the impact of such excesses on the fullness of debate. Ugly, hateful speech may force some participants to withdraw and may be as destructive to the full airing of an issue as speaking out of turn.

In conceiving of government as a parliamentarian, and suggesting that St. Paul's cross-burning ordinance might be seen as an instrument to further the robustness of public debate, I do not mean to ignore or slight the additional impact that cross-burning or similar expressive activities have upon the social standing of various groups. Indeed, I will even acknowledge the possibility that this was the motivating force behind the legislation. However, as some of the most honored cases teach, what is crucial for constitutional analysis is not the actual motive, but the possible justifications.[15] Regardless of the factors that subjectively moved the legislators, a law should be allowed to stand if it can be objectively justified—if it serves legitimate purposes. While standard First Amendment doctrine requires that the purpose of a regulation have special urgency (heightened scrutiny), and also that the fit between means and ends be more precise than usual (the least restrictive alternative), the validity of the law still turns on what might be said objectively in its defense.

Clearly, this mode of analyzing the St. Paul case depends upon specific facts and context. It turns upon a judgment as to whether the speech that is being regulated has a silencing effect and whether the robustness of public debate will be advanced by the state choosing the side that it does. On this score, it is hard to make blanket judgments. Even if the statute is limited to a narrow category of hateful speech, say "cross-burning," certain applications of the statute may be unconstitutional because, for example, the speech is aimed at someone who would not be silenced, as indeed might be the case if the target is not a member of a disadvantaged group. Then the hate speech may not have a silencing effect, and St. Paul may be unable to justify the application of the ordinance on the ground that it is acting like a parliamentarian. The silencing effects of words do not depend simply on their content, but also on the social standing of those who hear them.

For this reason, the decision of the Supreme Court in *R.A.V.* upholding the First Amendment rights of the perpetrators of this hateful act may be correct, but Scalia's underlying theory and the blanket condemnation of the ordinance are not. While I concede that there may be circumstances where hate speech does not have this silencing effect, and thus it would be impossible to justify the action of the state as a parliamentarian, the Court never attended to the consequences of hate speech upon discourse itself and thus never made the empirical inquiry such a theory requires. Seeing only a conflict between liberty and equality, and being determined to proclaim the priority of liberty, the Court struck down the statute on its face because it was partial. In doing this, the Court failed to understand that it was confronted not simply with a conflict between liberty and equality, but also with a conflict within liberty, and that in resolving such conflicts a certain measure of partiality may be acceptable and even necessary.

7

Free Speech and the Prior Restraint Doctrine

PROLOGUE

In the early 1980s, Burke Marshall was commissioned by the United States Information Service to put together a collection of essays that would introduce audiences abroad to the work of the Supreme Court. He invited me to join the project and I decided to focus on the Pentagon Papers case—one of the most celebrated encounters between the Supreme Court and the First Amendment. The choice of topic in part reflected the fact that I was immersed in the editing of the Kalven manuscript that later became A Worthy Tradition. *Also, a few years back, I had begun to examine the doctrine that figured so prominently in the case—the rule prohibiting prior restraints—as part of a more comprehensive treatment of remedies (see* The Civil Rights Injunction *(1978)).*

This essay does not explore the theme so central to all the others in this volume—the impact of social and economic inequalities on political liberties. It does, however, provide an important prelude to the issue to be explored in the next chapter—the needs of a free press. It also represents the first time I had to reflect systematically and critically on the work of my dear friend, Harry Kalven, who had, at a time when we were colleagues at the University of Chicago, commented on the Pentagon Papers case in the Foreword in the November 1971 Harvard Law Review. *In distancing myself from Kalven's hearty endorsement of the Court's decision in the case, I began to develop the critical disposition that would soon enough erupt in* Free Speech and Social Structure *(Chapter 1). The Marshall collection was published in 1982 under the title* The Supreme Court and Human Rights.

The 1960s was one of the finest moments for free speech in America. Citizens vigorously exercised their right to criticize the government, and the Supreme Court, under the leadership of Chief Justice Warren, protected the dissidents. The decade started with civil rights protests, but by the late 1960s the dissent largely focused on America's involvement in the Vietnam War.

The antiwar movement started with protests by fringe groups. As it became increasingly apparent that neither victory nor peace was at hand and that the United States was the primary combatant, not just a force supporting the South Vietnamese government, the protests came to embrace larger and larger sectors of the public. Soon the pressure was felt in electoral politics. The antiwar movement was responsible, arguably, for Lyndon Johnson's decision in 1968 not to seek reelection, the defeat in that year of Johnson's handpicked successor, Hubert Humphrey, and also for the candidacies during that era of Robert Kennedy, Eugene McCarthy, and George McGovern, all outspoken critics of the war.

The tactics of the antiwar movement also changed, from activity modeled after Martin Luther King's nonviolent civil rights protests to "confrontation politics"—mass gatherings that often took a disruptive and violent turn. Some of these confrontations, like the march on the Pentagon in 1967 and the demonstrations at the Democratic Convention in Chicago in 1968, are now part of our national history. The military draft was also attacked. Antiwar activists burnt their draft cards, urged resistance to the draft, invaded the offices of the Selective Service System, and often prevented the armed services from recruiting on college campuses. Private companies supplying material to the war effort became targets of protest activities, often of a brazen and vituperative character.

These tactics tested the limits of political tolerance. The free speech tradition in this country has never been a libertarian one. In every First Amendment case the task is to draw a line between protected and unprotected speech. The Supreme Court always sought to accommodate the state interest in maintaining order, and as the tactics of the antiwar movement became more disruptive, this interest pressed more heavily. The Warren Court commitment to fostering free and open debate was increasingly called into question.

I

On June 13, 1971, antiwar protest took a new turn and posed a new test for the free speech tradition. The *New York Times,* the most distinguished and respected of American newspapers, began publishing parts of the Pentagon Papers. The Papers, officially entitled *History of United States Decision-Making Process on Vietnam Policy,* was a voluminous history, consisting of 47 volumes, of the United States's role in Indochina. The study commissioned in 1967 by Robert McNamara, then the Secretary of Defense, took more than a year to complete. The persons who actually wrote the report had access to official government documents and communications, including material classified as top secret. The finished product consisted of a narrative (of about 3,000 pages) and a compilation of official documents (of about 4,000 pages). The Pentagon Papers was itself classified top secret.

The appearance of the Papers in the *New York Times* immediately caused a national stir and a reaction by Washington. The very next day, June 14, after the appearance of the second installment, the Attorney General of the United States sent the following telegram to the *Times:*

Arthur Ochs Sulzberger
President and Publisher
New York, New York

 I have been advised by the Secretary of Defense that the material published in The New York Times *on June 13, 14, 1971 captioned "Key Texts From Pentagon's Vietnam Study" contains information relating to the national defense of the United States and bears a top secret classification.*

 As such, publication of this information is directly prohibited by the provisions of the Espionage Law, Title 18, United States Code, Section 793.

 Moreover, further publication of information of this character will cause irreparable injury to the defense interests of the United States.

 Accordingly, I respectfully request that you publish no further information of this character and advise me that you have made arrangements for the return of these documents to the Department of Defense.

                                        John N. Mitchell
                                        Attorney General

What motivated this demand? This has remained a puzzling question, in large part because the Pentagon Papers was an historical document, covering the period from World War II until 1968. History can of course be embarrassing to an administration, but it is hard to see how *this* history—which stopped in 1968 and dealt mainly with the American military escalation during the Democratic presidencies of John Kennedy and Lyndon Johnson—could have been embarrassing to *this* administration, the Republican administration of Richard Nixon, which started in 1969. Conceivably the publication of the Papers might have interfered with the peace talks that were then in progress; publication could have, so it was said, strengthened the antiwar movement and thereby encouraged the Viet Cong or North Vietnam to be more intransigent. Or perhaps some of the documents, even though dated before 1968, might have revealed secrets about current military strategy or technology. But these explanations seem now, as they did then, far-fetched. As Justice Brennan emphasized in the case that later unfolded, at no time in the entire course of the litigation did the Attorney General make concrete his claim that publication would jeopardize "the defense interests of the United States." "The entire thrust of the Government's claim throughout these cases," the Justice said, "has been that publication of the material . . . 'could,' or 'might,' or 'may' prejudice the national interest in various ways."[1]

I suspect that the Attorney General was less concerned with the publication of this particular study than with the challenge to the *structure of authority*. Mitchell saw the publication of the Papers as a threat to the integrity of the classification system and the capacity of the administration to protect that system. That is why the concern was not confined to the *Times,* but also extended to Daniel Ellsberg, the RAND employee who worked on the Papers and made them available to the *Times* in defiance of their security classification. For the administration, Ellsberg's leaking of the Papers to the *Times,* and the *Times*'s decision to publish them, represented a threat not so much to the war effort in Indochina, but to the very power of the executive branch to maintain a measure of secrecy on issues relating to national defense.

The *Times,* of course, saw matters differently, and refused to comply with the Attorney General's demand to cease publication. In a statement that it made public, the *Times* claimed that it was "in the interest of the people of the country to be informed of the material contained in this series of articles." In saying this, the *Times* seemed to be indicating that it was prepared to run the risk of prosecution under the Espionage Act threatened in the telegram. It was taking the high road. But the *Times* reacted more meekly to the Attorney General's threat—made more explicit after the telegram was sent, but intimated in the sentence in the telegram that speaks about "irreparable injury"—to obtain an injunction against future publication. The *Times* said that it would resist in court the application for an injunction, but nevertheless "abide by the final decision of the court." In other words, the *Times* was prepared to run the risk of a criminal prosecution under the Espionage Act but not the risk of a contempt proceeding that might be brought for disobeying the injunction.

In the face of this divided response, and after the appearance of a third installment, the Attorney General made good on his threat to obtain an injunction against the *Times* and began a proceeding in the federal court in New York to that end. He was successful in the trial court, and although the *Times* appealed the decision to the Second Circuit, it ceased publication as promised. It appeared that the administration had scored an initial victory, but soon enough that injunction seemed to have little practical import. Some members of Congress obtained copies of the Papers and Senator Mike Gravel began reading them into the *Congressional Record.* The *Washington Post* also obtained a copy of the Papers and began publication. In response, the Attorney General commenced a suit against the *Washington Post* in a federal court in Washington. Unlike its New York counterpart, though, the trial court in Washington denied the injunction sought by the administration. That decision was affirmed by the Court of Appeals in the District of Columbia, while the Second Circuit affirmed the grant of injunction.

This odd pattern of decision led to two appeals in the Supreme Court. The Attorney General sought review of the Washington decision, while the *Times* sought review of the New York one. The court could not duck the issue and had little time to respond. The *Times* argued it was important for the people to have access to the Papers immediately and that it should be allowed to resume publication. The Attorney General was equally interested in a prompt resolution, for as each day passed, there was an increasing danger that his claim—at least as narrowly focused on the Pentagon Papers—would become moot: There would be no secrecy left to protect. Even after the appeals were docketed, the Papers started appearing in newspapers around the country, first in the *Boston Globe,* then in the *St. Louis Post-Dispatch,* then in the *Los Angeles Times.* The Court was also interested in a speedy disposition—it was about to recess for the summer.

In the face of this pressure, the Court expedited its consideration of the case. It issued stays to maintain the status quo in the Washington and New

York cases; it kept all the parties to tight briefing schedules; it even held a Saturday session for oral argument—all of which heightened the public attention on the case. On June 30, 1971, a little more than two weeks after the Papers first appeared in the press and the Attorney General brought suit, the Supreme Court announced its decision and rebuffed the Attorney General. Free speech won, but in a most curious way.

For one thing, the Court spoke with many voices. The nine Justices wrote nine separate opinions, though some joined the opinions of others, and their arguments broke into a number of different lines. Three of the justices—Burger, Harlan, and Blackmun—would have granted the Attorney General the injunction; they dissented. The other six Justices, who together constituted the majority, disagreed among themselves as to the grounds for denying the injunction. Justice Marshall invoked the concept of separation of powers. First, he argued, the executive should be confined to the traditional criminal law remedies provided by Congress; second, the courts were not free to "make law," as he believed would be entailed in issuing an injunction not specifically authorized by statute. The other five Justices also voted against the injunction, but they analyzed the case in free speech terms. They were, however, divided among themselves. Justices Black and Douglas took a libertarian stance: Freedom of speech is an absolute which tolerates no form of government censorship, whether it be in the form of an injunction or otherwise, whether it be in the name of national defense or less exalted purposes. The three other Justices who analyzed the case in free speech terms—Justices Brennan, Stewart, and White—fastened on the instrument of censorship sought: an injunction. They saw the injunction as a form of prior restraint, and read the First Amendment as an especially stringent prohibition against prior restraints.

Justice Brennan spoke most clearly on the high burden the government faced in justifying a prior restraint: "Thus, only governmental allegation and proof that publication must inevitably, directly, and immediately cause the occurrence of an event kindred to imperiling the safety of a transport already at sea can support even the issuance of an interim restraining order."[2] Justice Stewart similarly stated that a prior restraint would be tolerated only when the expression to be curbed would result "in direct, immediate, and irreparable damage to [the] Nation or its people."[3] He also implied that a lesser standard would be applied to so-called subsequent restraints—most ominously, maybe, the criminal prosecution the Attorney General was in fact threatening under the Espionage Act. Justice

White, the third of the Justices who invoked the prior restraint doctrine, was quite explicit on this point: "Prior restraints require an unusually heavy justification under the First Amendment; but failure by the Government to justify prior restraints does not measure its constitutional entitlement to a conviction for criminal publication. That the Government mistakenly chose to proceed by injunction does not mean that it could not successfully proceed in another way."[4] At the same time, he, unlike Brennan or Stewart, was strikingly silent about how stringent a standard was to be applied to prior restraints.

To compound matters, the Court also issued a tenth opinion, labeled "Per Curiam." Traditionally that label is saved for inconsequential opinions or orders, where there is no division among the Justices and where the point decided is so trivial as not to justify an extended discussion. In this instance, the Per Curiam had an entirely different function. It was used to locate a common point, or, to create a peg upon which the judgment of the Court—invalidating the injunction—could be hung.

In order to find common ground among the Justices, the Per Curiam opinion was strikingly sparse. It merely described the procedural posture of the cases before the Court, announced the result (setting aside the injunction), and justified that result with a very brief collection of quotes from some previous cases. The quotes made out the following syllogism: (1) Injunctions are prior restraints; (2) prior restraints require an especially stringent justification; (3) the Attorney General failed to meet that special burden of justification; (4) therefore, the injunction against the publication of the Pentagon Papers cannot stand.

Clearly the syllogism represented—in skeletal form—the position of Justices Brennan, Stewart, and White. Black and Douglas, the libertarians, subscribed to the conclusion (Step #4). They would go *at least* as far as indicated in the first three premises (Douglas's opinion, which Black joined, said so explicitly); it is just that they would apply the same standard to subsequent restraints. There is reason to believe that even the dissenters—Burger, Harlan, and Blackmun—subscribed to the first two premises, namely, the ones that honored the prior restraint doctrine. Those premises were amply supported by precedents, some new, some old, and a couple of years later, Chief Justice Burger, one of the dissenters, wrote of the Pentagon Papers case: "[E]very member of the Court, tacitly or explicitly, accepted the . . . condemnation of prior restraints as presumptively unconstitutional."[5] By this account, the disagreement of the dissenters centered only on the third premise, regarding the application of the doctrine in the case before them.

II

The Supreme Court decision was warmly received by the press and by the academic community. In an editorial the next day the *Times* characterized the Court's decision as "historic," "a ringing victory for freedom under law"; the *Times* said that "the nation's highest tribunal strongly reaffirmed the guarantee of the people's right to know." This is of course an exaggeration. As far as the Pentagon Papers themselves were involved, the Supreme Court's decision made little difference—by the time the Supreme Court acted, the Papers were already widely disseminated, a fact acknowledged in Justice White's opinion. Beyond the immediate issue of stopping publication of the Papers, the case offered the Court an opportunity to address important First Amendment issues and demarcate the bounds of free speech and the need for secrecy in national defense matters. On this level, the Supreme Court made virtually no contribution.

Long before the Court's decision, the subservience of the executive to the Constitution as construed by the Supreme Court was well established; it was never in doubt in this case. Indeed, the Attorney General implicitly honored this principle in turning to the courts to supply the instrument of censorship (the injunction). The Pentagon Papers case merely illustrated this tradition of judicial supremacy.

Similarly, the Court's treatment of the prior restraint doctrine broke no new constitutional ground. Just weeks before, the Court had invoked this doctrine to invalidate an injunction against the continuation of protest activity—picketing and pamphleteering—aimed at a real estate agent accused of "blockbusting."[6] At best, the Pentagon Papers case reaffirmed the prior restraint doctrine in a different context and in a highly visible fashion. But is *that* even cause for celebration?

Harry Kalven, the preeminent First Amendment scholar of that period, certainly thought so. In the 1971 Foreword to the *Harvard Law Review* he warmly praised the Court's decision and the prior restraint doctrine in general. He wrote, "What the Court appears to have decided in *Times* is that everything, or virtually everything, should be entitled to be published at least once." This view can, of course, be faulted on its value premise, that at least "virtually everything"—including a document bearing a "secret" or "top secret" classification—should be entitled to be published "at least once." One publication of a classified document is all that matters; nothing short of the libertarian position—rejected by the majority of the Court and by Kalven—would support such a devastating blow to the classification system. But even putting that issue to one side, Professor

Kalven's assessment of the significance of the case can be faulted on more technical, less normative grounds: The prior restraint doctrine provides for less adequate protection than Kalven would have us believe. Simply put, it does not provide that "virtually everything" is entitled to be published "at least once."

The prior restraint doctrine is essentially a comparative doctrine. It says that prior restraints are to be judged more stringently than subsequent restraints, but it does not say how stringent that higher standard is to be. Some of the Justices, notably Justices Stewart and Brennan, contemplated that on an absolute scale the standard for prior restraints was to be stringent indeed—similar to the near libertarian position that Black and Douglas would have applied to all constraints on publication, post or prior. Stewart and Brennan would have required for injunctions against speech a threat as "direct," "immediate," and "irreparable" as that imperiling a troop movement at sea (the well-known example used in *Near v. Minnesota*[7]). True, that standard would protect "virtually everything" from prior restraints. But that standard is not written into the Per Curiam, the decision of the Court—nor is any other standard, for that matter. The sparse Per Curiam speaks only in comparative terms.

To appreciate how malleable the prior restraint doctrine is, we need only note that Chief Justice Burger, who dissented in the Pentagon Papers case, later concluded that all Justices in that case embraced the prior restraint doctrine, and that the doctrine made all prior restraints "presumptively unconstitutional." How strong a presumption it was, or what it would take to rebut the presumption, he did not say. But he unwittingly provided two clues to his thinking. First, the Chief Justice himself was one of the three Justices who voted in the Pentagon Papers case itself to give the Attorney General his injunction. To permit such a result, the prescription must have been rather weak. The second clue to his thinking might be found in *Nebraska Press Ass'n v. Stuart*[8]—still another decision of the Chief Justice.

In *Nebraska Press*, a state court judge issued an injunction prohibiting the news media from reporting the confession of a man accused of murdering a family of six—a confession that had been made known in open court. The trial court feared that widespread prejudicial news coverage would imperil the accused's Sixth Amendment right to a fair trial by rendering impossible the impaneling of an impartial jury. Chief Justice Burger, writing for the majority, spoke approvingly of the prior restraint doctrine and the legacy of the Pentagon Papers case, yet he treated the discounted "clear and present danger" standard as the standard to be used to judge prior restraints. Under that test, the question is whether "the gravity of the 'evil,' discounted by its improbability, justifies such invasion of free speech as is necessary to avoid the danger."[9] In *Nebraska Press*, the Chief Justice held that the gag order failed to meet the requirements for a prior restraint because the lower court's conclusion as to the impact of the publicity on potential jurors was "speculative."[10] But given the gravity of the so-called "evil" invariably claimed in national security matters, that standard, which allows gravity to augment improbability, greatly strengthens the hand of the censor. Indeed, the discounted "clear and present danger" standard is one of the most infamous and least protective in the history of the First Amendment, even in the domain of subsequent restraints. Suffice it to say that it made possible the conviction of the Communist leaders in the McCarthy era. Indeed, the invocation of that test by Chief Justice Burger led Justices Brennan and Stewart to strongly disassociate themselves from the Chief Justice's opinion in *Nebraska Press*, even though they agreed with the ultimate result.[11]

While it is true that Chief Justice Burger was one of the dissenters in the Pentagon Papers case, his *Nebraska Press* gloss on the that decision cannot be easily dismissed on that ground. Justice White, one of the five who joined the Pentagon Papers case Per Curiam, also joined the Chief Justice's opinion in *Nebraska Press*, though not without some hesitation—he also found it necessary to write a short separate opinion. In the Pentagon Papers case Justice White explicitly argued that prior restraints should be held to a higher standard than subsequent restraints and that in the present instance that higher standard was not met. But he took no position as to how stringent the prior restraint standard should be. By signing on to Chief Justice Burger's opinion in *Nebraska Press*, Justice White answered the question: not very.[12]

Professor Kalven's assessment of the Pentagon Papers case can thus be faulted on the ground that it incorrectly assumes a high near-absolute standard for prior restraints. That assumption is not securely rooted in the Court's opinion—the Per Curiam—and it is in fact contradicted by subsequent cases, specifically *Nebraska Press*. Professor Kalven also failed to question the Court's highly formalistic definition of the category of prior restraints. The Court included injunction but excluded criminal statutes, allowing the latter to be treated as subsequent restraints and to be judged by the lesser applicable standard. In doing this, the Court ignored the structural similarity between injunctions and criminal statutes.[13]

In order to see the structural similarity, a distinction must be drawn between two distinct phases of the injunctive process, issuance and enforcement. In its issuance phase, the injunction resembles a criminal statute: It establishes a standard of conduct and threatens to punish those who disobey. It controls through deterrence. An injunction is often classified as a prior restraint because it can be issued before publication. That only means that the injunction controls—deters—before the event to be avoided—here publication—actually occurs. But that is equally true of the criminal statute. It restrains before publication; it deters future conduct. The criminal prosecution takes place after the event, after publication, but that phase of the criminal process should be compared to the enforcement phase of the injunctive process—the contempt proceeding. In each case, sanctions are imposed on those who violate the standard of conduct. Contempt and criminal prosecution are retrospective; an injunction and a criminal statute are both preventive.

In the Pentagon Papers case the Supreme Court was confronted with an injunction, not a criminal statute. But by choosing to rely on the prior restraint doctrine—thereby introducing a double standard, more demanding for prior restraints and less demanding for subsequent restraints—and by taking a formalistic view of what constitutes a prior restraint—injunctions, not criminal statutes—the Court left the criminal statute unencumbered. It left the Espionage Act in effect, fully capable of deterring access and publication. The government's classification system thus remained protected by a legal instrument as powerful as the injunction. Kalven's enthusiasm notwithstanding, the Pentagon Papers case did not establish that "virtually everything" is entitled to be published "at least once." Everything could be published at least once, that's true—but only if the publisher were willing to face prosecution down the road—as would be the case if an injunction were issued.

There are, of course, differences between injunctions and criminal statutes, even viewing both as preventive instruments. For example, the injunction is likely to be more specific in terms of the act prohibited and the persons addressed; if the injunction is violated, the judge has the power to initiate the criminal contempt proceeding; there is no jury in criminal contempt if the punishment turns out to be a petty one (e.g., less than six months imprisonment); the range of defenses to an injunction may be more limited. On the basis of these differences Professor Kalven viewed the injunction as a more potent or more dangerous instrument of censorship than the statute and concluded that it should be subjected to a more stringent First Amendment standard. I am more skeptical.[14]

First, the purported differences between injunctions and criminal statutes might not exist in fact. Although injunctions often have a specificity not found in criminal statutes, in this instance the Espionage Act was rendered more specific by the very explicit and concrete threat contained in the Attorney General's telegram. Prosecutorial threats are not at all unusual in cases of this type. Second, some of the attributes of the injunction that allegedly differentiate it from a criminal statute may well further First Amendment values, and thus may not just be a preferable form of sanction. Specificity, for example, curtails or eliminates the chilling effect that comes from vague or overbroad statutes. The fact that "prosecutorial discretion" in criminal contempt is vested in a judge rather than a political officer, the Attorney General, also serves as an added layer of protection for speech. The Attorney General is likely to be more sensitive to the pressures of the majority or the political needs of the administration he or she serves—pressures the First Amendment is supposed to guard against. Third, some of the so-called strengths of the injunction as a deterrent instrument are offset by other factors. The specificity of the injunction and the absence of the jury might, for instance, enhance the likelihood of a punishment being imposed for violating an injunction, as opposed to violating a statute; on the other hand, the anticipated penalty for violating an injunction is usually petty, especially compared to that likely to be imposed for violating a criminal statute—in this instance, a $10,000 fine and ten years in prison. The deterrent effect of a legal instrument is a product of *both* the certainty *and* the severity of the anticipated sanction.

It is true that in this particular case, the *Times* was willing to run the risk of criminal prosecution under the Espionage Act but not that of contempt of the injunction: Recall the *Times*'s divided response to John Mitchell's telegram. But the response of the *Times* probably had little to do with the respective deterrent powers of the injunction and the Act. Rather, it was probably more a reflection of the dual institutional roles of the *Times*, both advocate of a free press and responsible corporate citizen, and of its willingness to take on the political branch, but not the judiciary. It is unlikely, however, that others prepared to engage in radical criticism of governmental policies would feel similarly divided. The *Times* itself never gave a satisfactory account of its decision. In fact, in a public address later that fall, the newspaper's general counsel recognized that the promise to obey the injunction was ill-conceived.[15] In subsequent cases the *Times* reserved to itself the right to decide whether it would obey an injunction directed against publication.

Professor Kalven, in one final attempt to locate the achievement of the Pentagon Papers case, suggested that the divided response of the *Times*— whatever its basis—might have given the prior restraint doctrine a special attractiveness in that particular case, as a means for preserving "the chance for civil disobedience." The *Times* was prepared to violate the Espionage Act in the name of the people's right to know, but not the injunction. But surely by the time the Supreme Court rendered its decision that moment for civil disobedience had already passed. Daniel Ellsberg had already obtained possession of the Papers and made them available to the *Times*. The *Times* might have been prepared to abide by the final outcome of the litigation and to hold up publication until the case was finally decided, but others were not. The Papers were widely disseminated as the litigation wound its way through the courts. When the Supreme Court finally spoke, the Papers were fully in the public domain. The issue before the Court was not whether the opportunity for Ellsberg or the *Times* to engage in civil disobedience should be preserved; that opportunity had already expired. The true issue was the general *structure of authority,* the integrity of the classification system, and the Supreme Court left that structure very much intact.

In the months following the Court's decision, the Attorney General made good on his threat to use the Espionage Act. In the summer of 1971, grand juries were convened. As it turned out, the *Times* was not indicted, nor were any of its officers or reporters. We will never know why that occurred, whether the Attorney General decided not to seek an indictment against the *Times* or whether the grand jury balked, or what the grounds of that action might have been. Some might attribute the good fortune of the *Times* to the Supreme Court's decision in the Pentagon Papers case, not the formal terms of decision, but the simple outcome of that case, which might have made it politically difficult for the administration to obtain or even seek an indictment against the *Times* for having published the Papers. The popular mind might well read the Supreme Court as having "allowed" the *Times* to publish the Papers. We will never know whether that conjecture is right. What we do know, however, is that Daniel Ellsberg was indicted and fully prosecuted under the Espionage Act. Ultimately, that prosecution was dismissed, but not on account of the Pentagon Papers case or free speech considerations. Rather, the dismissal was due to wholly collateral circumstances—overreaching by the government in the conduct of its prosecution (e.g., breaking into Ellsberg's psychiatrist's office to obtain evidence; offering the directorship of the FBI to the trial judge), which, to give our story one further twist, was to figure in the impeachment proceedings brought against Richard Nixon in 1974.

In the end, the Pentagon Papers case must be seen as a victory for free speech—the Court ruled on the right side of the issue. But in my judgment it was neither a "ringing victory" nor a "strong reaffirmation" of "the people's right to know." Rather, a transitional Court, newly under the leadership of Chief Justice Warren Burger but still staffed by Black, Douglas, Brennan, and Marshall—simply built on the accomplishments of the previous era. The Warren Court had significantly changed the domain of free speech in the United States, and it was the legacy of that tribunal that helped give the *Times,* Daniel Ellsberg, and the antiwar movement the courage, and maybe even the impetus, to do what they did. The Pentagon Papers case gave dramatic expression to the Warren Court legacy. It did so, however, only by the power of its ultimate outcome—by denying the Attorney General's request, not by invoking the prior restraint doctrine.

III

The prior restraint doctrine received an important statement in the 1930s in *Near v. Minnesota*. For the next 40 years it maintained a very low profile; in fact during the fifteen years of the Warren Court it was virtually invisible. But during the 1970s it became a favorite of the Burger Court, and became an increasingly important part of the free speech jurisprudence of that institution.[16] What might account for this development? Part of the answer is suggested by the Pentagon Papers case itself and the role the doctrine played in that case.

The prior restraint doctrine is distinguished by its ambivalence. On the one hand, it holds injunctions to a higher standard than criminal statutes; on the other hand, it does not specify how high that standard is on an absolute scale, nor does it provide protection against other preventive instruments, such as criminal statutes, even though they may be equally effective in deterring speech. From a purely analytic perspective this ambivalence may seem to be a failing, an incoherence, but on another level this ambivalence only increased the appeal of the doctrine to a divided Court drifting to the Right. The ambivalent analytic structure of the doctrine enhanced its strategic utility.[17] There was something for everyone.

Justices from the right wing of the Court, presumably more responsive to the state's interest in limiting speech, would be comforted by the continued operation of the criminal statute. They would also be able to pay homage to the First Amendment, wrap themselves up in the emotive force attaching to the traditional ban on prior restraints, and then fill the empty vessel of the prior restraint doctrine—the essentially comparative standard—with a content that could be, on an absolute scale, as restrictive as they wished. As Chief Justice Burger was anxious to remind us, even the dissenters in the Pentagon Papers case subscribed to the prior restraint doctrine.

A Justice from the more liberal wing would of course be concerned with the gaps, the silences of the doctrine, and view them as implied concessions to the power of the censor. Such a Justice might wish to impose a standard on subsequent restraints that was as high as that on prior restraints; Justices Black and Douglas indeed tried to do that in the Pentagon Papers case, as did Justice Brennan on other occasions in the heyday of the Warren Court (for example, in constructing his overbreadth doctrine). But once it was recognized, as it must have been in the Pentagon Papers case, that this position was not likely to be adopted by a majority, the liberal Justices would have no interest in repudiating the prior restraint doctrine. It may have been their only hope. Indeed, a liberal judge—such as Brennan—might even have proposed prior restraint as a basis of decision, as a compromise candidate, as a way of obtaining the votes from the middle of the Court.

For Justices in the ideological center of the Court—people like White and Stewart—the prior restraint doctrine also offered a doctrinal way out of their quandary. These Justices were more committed to free speech than the conservatives, but at the same time they were more respectful than liberals of the countervalues advanced by the state—the interests threatened by the speech, in this instance the classification system and the need of national defense. The prior restraint doctrine did not resolve that ambivalence but rather served it, for the doctrine itself is ambivalent. A decision against censorship predicated on the prior restraint doctrine is a divided or weak rebuff to the censor, denying *only* the injunction without a comparable restriction on the criminal sanction and without a ringing endorsement of free speech values. The weakness of the rebuff would be attractive to a Justice from the middle of the Court, for it would express his own view of the merits, and though it would be a source of concern to the liberals, a weak "no" would be seen by him as a lot better than a "yes," a decision approving the censorship.

The prior restraint doctrine thus should not be seen as a full or coherent expression of free speech values, but rather as a strategic device capable of effectuating a compromise, the chief value of which is negative—to block a decision against speech. The Pentagon Papers case might itself not have been a great victory for speech, but the opposite result, a decision le-gitimating the Attorney General's demand for silence—a chilling and in-deed plausible thought given the closeness of the division—would have been a devastating blow to the First Amendment. Like the war, that deci-sion had to be stopped, no matter what the terms.

8
Building
a Free Press

PROLOGUE

In the rush of events following the collapse of the Berlin Wall in 1989, more and more attention focused on the United States Supreme Court and the body of decisions it had produced. To the world, the United States appeared the most stable and vibrant of all democracies, and many thought that one of the keys to its success lay in the role that the Supreme Court had created for itself. Comparative constitutional law became a growth industry. To a large extent, I welcomed this development, believing that there was a lot in the history of the Supreme Court of which we could be proud. Nonetheless, I worried that in the climate of the late 1980s and the 1990s, dominated by an exaltation of capitalism as expounded by Ronald Reagan and Margaret Thatcher, the wrong lessons might be extracted from our constitutional experience. This was the dominant theme of the seminar I taught with George Priest in the early 1990s entitled "Capitalism or Democracy?"

Ever since Hungary broke from the Soviet bloc and established a constitutional democracy, it has been besieged by problems in its efforts to create a free press, especially in the broadcasting field. It was therefore natural that the first major conference in the region on issues regarding freedom of the press was held in Budapest. The conference was convened in June 1993 by the Central European University in that city and was attended by representatives of the countries from the former Soviet empire as well as by scholars from the United States, Germany, and England. This essay was written for that conference and first appeared in the Spring 1995 issue of the Yale Journal of International Law. *Reflecting a slant much to my liking, the title of the conference was "The Development of Rights of Access to the Media"; but, as reflected in this essay, I believe access should be regarded as a second-generation issue—to be addressed after one has gotten the basic structure right.*

The year 1989 marked a new beginning. The Berlin Wall fell, and with it, the Soviet empire. East Germany was soon absorbed by the Federal Republic of Germany, but other nations in Central and Eastern Europe long held in captivity by the Soviet Union proclaimed their independence. History took still another turn in 1991. The Soviet Union itself disintegrated, and from its ruins a great many new nations emerged in Central Asia and Eastern Europe.

All the nations that once constituted the Soviet Union and its empire are now engaged in a reconstructive process of considerable scope and intensity. One dimension of this reconstructive process is economic: The great socialist experiment, in which all the means of production were owned by the state, has been declared a failure. The production of goods and services under socialism lagged behind that of capitalist societies, and in the name of economic efficiency reformers are now transferring the ownership of state enterprises to private hands.

Another facet of the reconstructive process is political. Many former Soviet-bloc countries have denounced their totalitarian past and have, often through the adoption of a new constitution, committed themselves to democratic principles—to making government responsive to the desires and wishes of the citizens instead of the other way around.

In many respects, the economic and political facets of the reconstructive process are consistent with one another. Indeed, economic reforms may facilitate the establishment of democracy and are often justified in those terms. Removing the power over economic decisions such as jobs and income from the hands of government officials not only improves efficiency, but also deprives these officials of a powerful instrument of control over the public. Citizens will feel freer to criticize and disagree. Of course, state officials can still retaliate against citizen-critics by launching criminal prosecutions. Criminal sanctions are more visible, however, and thus perhaps harder to deploy than economic decisions like deciding not to hire or promote someone. In any event, criminal sanctions were already available under a socialist economy.

From this perspective, the task of building a free press in the new democracies is rather straightforward. Transfer ownership of all the state-owned media—both the newspapers and the electronic media—to private interests. Sell, or simply give away, assets like printing presses and broadcast facilities. Allow free entry of new media enterprises. In some domains, licenses may be necessary to avoid interferences on broadcasting frequencies due to spectrum scarcity, but such licenses can be awarded to the highest bidders or through a lottery. In no case should they be reserved for supporters of the regime.

This program of rapid privatization would bring economic gains to the new regime, but even more significantly from democracy's perspective, it would enhance the independence of the media from government officials. Newspapers, television, and radio would then be able to provide citizens with a range of information and opinions on the actions of the government, including some fiercely critical. For the first time, citizens would be in a position to choose their representatives in an informed manner and to force state officials to respond to the desires of the public.

One hitch may arise from the fact that the reporters and journalists working for the newly privatized media are likely to be the same ones who worked for the state-owned media in the past. Changes in ownership do not immediately produce a change in personnel. Additional efforts may be necessary to overcome the effects of life in a totalitarian society, which is likely to have dulled or destroyed the critical faculties of journalists who served the dictatorship.[1] Reporters and other journalists must therefore be encouraged to use the privileges of freedom purchased for them by private capital. Journalists may also need to organize themselves and elevate journalism into an honorable profession, independent of the state and devoted to making government policies responsive to citizens' desires.

In time, state officials might retaliate or sanction outspoken critics in the newly privatized press. Such actions might take criminal or civil forms. State officials might charge particular journalists or broadcasters with lessening the esteem of the state (seditious libel), destroying the reputations of individual public officials (defamation), disclosing state secrets (subversion), or even fomenting unrest (inciting a breach of the peace).[2] Such state actions are not necessarily mean-spirited or vindictive. They often are intended to protect legitimate state interests—for example, maintaining public order or ensuring the smooth functioning of government. Nevertheless, in order to permit the press freely to criticize government—to provide what has been called "breathing space"[3]—these retaliatory actions by the state against the newly privatized media should be strictly restrained.

How might this be done? We in the United States have struggled with this question for some time now in a setting where the press is almost entirely privately owned, and we have hit on a solution that may be instructive. We have adopted a written constitution that guarantees freedom of the press, and turned to the judiciary—an institution that stands above the fray of partisan politics and insulated from sanctions by the political branches—to enforce that law. As a result, legal doctrine has emerged that confers a certain measure of autonomy on the press. This autonomy varies from context to context, depending on the political value of the speech and the strength of the countervailing state interest in curbing speech. Small, tentative gestures in the same direction have appeared in the new democracies of the East, most notably Hungary.[4] They should be encouraged, though they will not be enough.

I

Underlying the general strategy I have been outlining for building a free press—privatizing the press, encouraging journalists to see themselves as members of a profession, and creating for the press a constitutionally protected zone of autonomy from state regulation—is an assumption that the state is the natural enemy of democracy. Indeed, aside from the purely economic considerations, privatization recommends itself so strongly as a democratic strategy because it takes control of the press away from the state. Such an assumption about the unfriendly posture of the state is most understandable in a transitional democracy, where people have lived under a state dictatorship for many years and are now trying to escape from that horror. The transition occurring in the former Soviet empire, however, will not last forever. In any event, memories of the immediate past should not obscure the full dimensions of the reconstructive process. For more than two hundred years the United States has had a continuous democracy, and in this setting we have learned that the state can have two faces—sometimes it acts as an enemy of democracy, sometimes as its friend.

This view of the state may initially seem paradoxical, a replay of the double-talk that characterized the socialist dictatorships of the not-too-distant past. The role of the state in protecting democracy becomes clear, however, once it is understood that the market is itself a structure of constraint. Although the newly privatized press might be called "free" because the state does not own or control the papers or radio and television stations, the media do not operate in a social vacuum. Owners will seek to maximize profits by maximizing revenue and minimizing costs, and competitive pressure will curb their capacity to maximize revenue. These are the iron laws of capitalist economics; they will hold true for the newly privatized press just as they do for any other business. The state might therefore be needed to counteract those constraints placed on the press by the market.

No social actor is completely autonomous. Everyone is embedded in a social structure and is constrained by it. A question must thus be asked whether, from a purely political perspective, the constraints imposed by the market on the media are of any special concern. Those most devoted to privatization argue that these constraints are not inconsistent with democratic goals and indeed might actually further such goals. The desire to maximize revenue will drive publishers and broadcasters to increase the attractiveness of their product to the public and thus make the coverage and method of presentation responsive to consumer desires. The public gets what it wants. Economic theory and the American experience demonstrate the force behind this view, but I do not believe it conveys the whole story.

First, costs will limit the capacity of the newly privatized media to respond to consumer desires. Entrepreneurs seek to maximize profits, which, as noted earlier, requires minimizing costs as well as maximizing revenues. Therefore, the media may well offer the public considerably less than it wants. Overwhelmed by the costs of gathering the news or producing high-quality documentaries, leaders in the television industry will be tempted, for example, to rely on reruns of sitcoms or soap operas. Of course, this may be all that some sector of the public wants. But some viewers may be frustrated and others may simply lower their expectations and adapt their preferences to what is available.

Second, reliance on advertising as the method of generating revenue— typical wherever the press is privatized—will introduce the same type of distortions that have occurred in the United States. One such distortion stems from the obvious fact that regardless of how much the public desires a program or series of articles, advertisers will not underwrite these programs or articles unless they are likely to enhance the sales of the would-be advertisers' products. Some reporters claimed, for example, that the commercial television networks in the United States slighted coverage of the Gulf War because advertisers did not want their products associated with scenes of death and destruction.[5]

The power of advertisers over the content of the press is not confined to such deliberate or discrete interventions. As a general matter, advertisers will use a particular newspaper or television show only if it is likely to be viewed or read by people who have the money, taste, and inclination to buy their products, and publishers and broadcasters will shape their product to appeal to those persons. As a result, particular "target audiences," not the public in general, are the special concerns of the privately owned press, and privately owned newspapers or broadcast facilities may neglect the informational and cultural needs of groups whose purchasing power is weak or for whom advertising will have less of a payoff.

Third, while a certain segment of the public may govern the content of broadcasts and newspapers through ordinary market processes, these individuals do not make that choice through a process of collective deliberation. Rather, they act atomistically, and this mode of interaction may have profound consequences for the statement and definition of their preferences. The radio or television programs that individuals choose in the privacy of their homes, after dinner and a day's work, might well be different than the programs they would choose after fully discussing and debating all the options. The same is true regarding the daily purchase of a newspaper. In repudiating the dictatorships of the past and turning to democracy, eighty-niners have not committed themselves to deliberating collectively about each and every social decision, nor does democratic theory require such a commitment. However, the normative force of any claim made in the name of "the public"—in this case concerning the coverage of the press—often presupposes such deliberation.

Thus, there is good reason to doubt that the newly privatized media will give the public all that it wishes. Coverage or broadcasts determined by the market—what I will call "market-determined speech"—will only be a rough approximation of "democratically determined speech," the broadcasts and coverage that a people would choose after full deliberation, unconstrained by costs, and governed by the principle of one person/one vote.[6] There may be, however, a deeper source of concern: Should the ideal or standard by which one judges the output of the market be what I have called democratically determined speech? Democracy involves a choice by a people about the type of government and society they desire, but perhaps that choice does not extend to the views that they should hear or the positions that they must confront in making these other choices. Perhaps the aspirations should be even higher.

Democracy is a system of government that ultimately allows the public to decide how it wishes to live. It is predicated on the principle of collective self-determination and as a necessary corollary presupposes that in making its judgment the public is fully apprised of the options available and the conflicting points of view on any issue. Otherwise the public is not in a position to decide what is in its best interest or how it might further those interests; it is not determining its own fate. Within this framework, the function of a free press is to provide the public with the information it needs to exercise its sovereign prerogative. One way of expressing this idea is to say that the mission of the press in a democratic system, whether in one of the new democracies of the East or in an established democracy such as the United States, is to produce on matters of public importance a debate that is "uninhibited, robust, and wide-open."[7]

Suppose the people decide, however, that they are sick and tired of "robust public debate," exhausted by discussions over economic policy or the treatment of ethnic minorities, and are only interested in mind-dulling entertainment, tabloid newspapers, or television programs that give expression to their sexual fantasies. Would a democracy require us to respect that choice? I think not, no more than a commitment to contractual freedom would require us to respect a contract by which someone sells himself or herself into slavery.

A distinction should thus be drawn between "democratically determined speech" and what I have called "robust public debate," and the latter should be the standard against which we measure the output of the market. Such a view may seem alien to the system of liberties we have traditionally associated with democratic governments, but it is not. The American Bill of Rights, including the protection afforded to the press in the First Amendment, is often spoken of as a protection of "minority rights" or "individual rights," or as a bulwark against the "tyranny of the majority."[8] In protecting the press against state interference, the Supreme Court knows all too well that often the state is not acting against the will of the majority but rather as an instrument of that will. The Court has imposed upon itself a responsibility to preserve the robustness of public debate—in other words, to protect democracy from itself.

In a similar vein, then, the nation builders of the East should be concerned with constraints imposed by the market, not simply because market-determined speech will be a poor approximation of democratically determined speech, but rather because it may well depart significantly from the more abstract, largely idealized standard of robust public debate. Once the media are privatized, programming and coverage will be largely determined by the confluence of a number of factors—marginal cost and marginal revenue, for example—that have no discernible relationship to the needs of a democratic polity. Having committed their capital, the owners of the media are likely to have their minds on profits, not on the task of supplying the public with the information and opinions it needs in order to exercise its democratic prerogative.

Even accepting this view, some may treat state constraints on public debate as being on a wholly different plane than constraints emanating from the market. This position is commonplace in the United States. To some extent its currency derives from the precise wording of our guarantee of freedom of the press: "Congress shall make no law abridging the freedom of speech, or of the press."[9] Conceived in these terms, the distinction often drawn by American lawyers between the constraints of the state and those of the market may not be relevant to those now actively engaged in the process of building new democratic societies, because they may be drafting new constitutions or interpreting constitutional provisions worded in more affirmative terms. For example, the new Hungarian constitution, following the European tradition, states that "[t]he Republic of Hungary shall recognize and protect freedom of the press."[10] My own impression, however, is that the American distinction between market constraints and state constraints actually rests on grounds that are more philosophic than textual, and thus is likely to have a broader appeal.

One justification for drawing a distinction between market and state constraints construes the domain of public debate narrowly and confines it to speech that pertains to elections for public office or the work of government.[11] The democratic mission of the press, so the argument runs, is to assist the public in choosing government officials and evaluating their work; the principal danger is that government officials will use their power to retaliate against those who dare to criticize them.

In my view, however, there is no reason to construe the democratic mission of the press so narrowly. Certainly, the press should "check" government officials, to borrow Professor Blasi's term,[12] but it also has a responsibility to address large questions of economic and social structure such as the distribution of wealth and the role of workers in the management of their firms. All such subjects are within the jurisdiction of the electorate in a democratic society.

Moreover, even if the domain of public debate is conceived narrowly, thereby limiting it to criticism of government officials and their policies, there still may be reason to fear market constraints because they have the effect of favoring certain government policies and the officials who implement them. Imagine the position a newly privatized press, necessarily relying on huge infusions of private capital, would take on a political candidate urging a radical redistribution of wealth or the institution of worker control.[13] Although not every government policy is market-sensitive in this way, many are; there is thus reason for concern about the impact of market constraints on public debate even if the concern is confined only to speech that considers government affairs.

State constraints and market constraints have also been sharply differentiated because they are enforced by different methods.[14] The state has a monopoly over the legitimate use of force and can throw those who violate its edicts in jail. Media moguls enforce their demands by excluding an article, shaping a show in a certain way, or firing a reporter who turns in copy that does not sell papers. In actual practice, however, this distinction between enforcement methods may be less clear-cut. The state can enforce its constraints through civil remedies (e.g., damage awards or denial of licenses); if the United States is any guide, such remedies may well become commonplace. The presumed difference in the harshness of the sanctions is also questionable. How much worse is it to throw someone in jail than for a person to be fired or have his or her business fail? Yet even if we allow for these distinctions, the different methods by which the state and market enforce their edicts is not significant from democracy's perspective. What matters is not the moral quality of the means used to enforce a constraint or the hardship suffered by the individual who bears the brunt of the sanction, but rather the effect of the constraint upon public discourse.

II

Reformers of the East must be as aware of the market constraints on the press as they are of state constraints. Rapid privatization, buttressed by judicial doctrine declaring the autonomy of the press and a professional ethos promoting independence from the state, should remain the overall strategy. Privatization is necessary to eradicate the traditions of suppression that the dictatorial practices of the past may have created. But the reformers must not stop at that point. They must also contemplate a wide number of interstitial strategies to counteract the constraining effect of the market.

Although crafting these strategies will be a daunting responsibility for the eighty-niners, they may find some guidance in the experience of this country, which for many years has accepted private ownership for the basic economic structure of the media but supplemented that structure in a number of ways. We have experimented with two types of supplemental regulations; one might be called "program regulation," the other "structural regulation."

Program regulation directly controls the content of broadcasts or publications for purposes of broadening the viewpoints available to the public. Examples include the Federal Communications Commission's (FCC) "fairness doctrine," which requires broadcasters to cover issues of public importance and to do so fairly.[15] Another example would be laws granting persons subject to personal or political attack a "right of reply,"[16] and requirements that the networks give adequate coverage to presidential elections.[17] At one time public interest groups attempted to have the FCC require networks to air "editorial advertisements."[18] This too might be considered a program regulation.

Structural regulations serve the same end, though they work more indirectly. Antitrust laws are an example of structural regulation, though they are limited in that they seek to perfect the market rather than to counteract it.[19] A more robust variant appears in the "cross-ownership" rules of the FCC, which prohibit the owner of a newspaper from acquiring a television or radio station in the same market.[20] Sometimes such acquisitions are barred even though they pose no threat to the smooth functioning of a competitive market. The justification is political, not economic. An even more significant form of structural regulation is Congress's decision in the 1960s to establish and fund a public broadcasting network that was to supplement rather than supplant the commercial networks.[21] Such a public broadcasting system could cover issues likely to be slighted by the commercial networks but nevertheless vital to democratic self-government.[22] Finally, mention should be made of the FCC's policy of giving preference to racial minorities in awarding broadcast licenses.[23] To some extent, the policy can be understood as a way of improving the social status of minorities; yet it also has a speech dimension and can therefore be considered a form of structural regulation. This view assumes that race is a proxy for viewpoint, and that the new owners will exercise discretion allowed to them by the market in favor of diversifying programming and thus enriching public debate.

Although the regulatory measures I have just described are aimed mainly at television and radio, as opposed to the print media, they can be adapted to the newspaper industry. The Supreme Court has accepted some legal constraints on newspapers (for example, in the antitrust context), but it has generally been hostile to any regulation of newspapers and has built into the law a distinction between electronic and print media. Most notably, the Court invalidated a Florida right-to-reply statue that presumably would have been constitutional if applied to broadcasters.[24] This distinction is difficult to justify, however, and those trying to create a new constitutional framework for their countries might safely ignore this odd feature of our law.

Newspapers are part of the working press, as are television and radio stations. All shape public discourse and inform people of the world that lies beyond their immediate experience. Broadcast television and radio stations must receive licenses from the state in order to avoid interferences on the electromagnetic spectrum. Cable television and radio stations transmit their signals over wires, but they might also need a system of licensing to preserve the integrity of public streets or spaces, in much the same manner as does a telephone system.[25] There is, however, no physical imperative for the licensing of newspapers. Consequently, a distinction between the electronic and print media may be thought to arise from the way property rights are created. The property rights of a television or radio station have their origins in a deliberate, allocative decision of government, specifically the award of a license. The property rights of newspapers have a more diffuse origin; they come from laws that apply to all businesses. However, the special status of the press and its claim for freedom derive from the function of that institution in society—to inform the public—and should not turn on the source of its property rights or the particular dynamics that gave rise to them.[26]

The supplemental state interventions I have described seek to enrich rather than impoverish public debate and are generally referred to under the category of the "right of access." This term, introduced into American constitutional discourse by an influential article in the late 1960s by Professor Jerome Barron,[27] seeks to capitalize on the mystique that surrounds "rights-talk" in the United States. The term is misleading for that very reason, however. While most of the rights that figure in contemporary constitutional debates, for instance, the right to procreative freedom, further some individualistic value, properly understood Barron's "right of access" does not attempt to protect the self-expressive interests of an individual citizen seeking access. Rather, it is intended to further a social goal: the production of robust public debate. A more apt expression—and the one I will use to refer to the entire panoply of program and structural regulations that seek to enrich public debate—is "access regulations."

Even with this emendation, an ambiguity persists. People speak of access, but they do not specify access to what. Because the purpose of access regulations is to enrich public discourse, rather than to give vent to some self-expressive interest of the individual, what must be guaranteed is access to the public, not access to a medium. Access to a radio or television station or newspaper is only a means of affording access to the public, and any access regulation should be judged accordingly. For this reason, the so-called public access channels commonly found on American cable television are inadequate. The person appearing on television at 3:00 A.M. may feel some measure of personal satisfaction, but what he or she says plays no more role in public deliberations than does a book buried deep in the stacks of a university library. Of course, a would-be listener can seek out the viewpoint, but one must be realistic about the public's inquisitiveness. On the other hand, as long as the viewpoint or information is in general circulation and thus fully available to the public, no further demand for access can be made. The predicate for regulation dissolves, and to insist upon access in these circumstances would be unnecessary, perhaps even vindictive. To use a metaphor of Charles Fried, it would be "a way of showing off power by hoisting flags on other people's flagpoles."[28]

Viewed broadly, then, the American constitutional experience has two sides. To fulfill its democratic mission, the press must have a measure of autonomy from the state, but that autonomy must never preclude access regulations. The basic structure should be privately owned, but some state subsidies are appropriate to create television or radio stations and even opinion journals that are not totally controlled by the market. Legal doctrine must protect the press from state regulations that stifle public debate (e.g., prosecutions for seditious libel), but not those that have the opposite effect (e.g., the fairness doctrine). As a matter of professional ethics, journalists must maintain their independence from the state, without identifying too closely with the economic goals of the enterprises for which they work. At every turn, the press must inform people of the issues before them and present the conflicting and diverse views on those issues. Only then will citizens be in a position to exercise the prerogative that democracy promises.

III

The risk is great that eighty-niners will ignore the multifaceted quality of the American constitutional experience. The reformers may come to believe that freedom of the press requires no more than autonomy from the state, ignoring the need for access regulations. This misreading of the American experience may have many sources, including the activism of international monetary organizations. More likely, this belief will derive from an odd fortuity of timing: The reconstruction is being undertaken at a time when the validity of access regulations in this country is most suspect. During the 1960s and early 1970s, Americans understood the importance of access regulations. Over the next two decades, however, the activist state fell into disfavor and we became more and more obsessed with the wonders of the market. As a result, the "right of access" and the entire idea of regulating the press in the name of democracy came under increasing attack. I fear that eighty-niners, like all politicians, may have limited time horizons and confuse the Reagan years with the whole of the American experience.

Looking to America to guide them in the reconstructive endeavor, the eighty-niners will therefore need a broad historical perspective. They will also require a measure of critical discernment to assess the many objections that were raised to access regulations during the 1970s and 1980s. One such objection arose from a doubt about whether such regulations actually enriched public debate. Some argued that the fairness doctrine made the networks more timid about what they chose to broadcast, for fear that if they carried a controversial show, they would need to allow time for a response. The effect of regulation, the claim went, was a form of self-censorship—gray speech.

On the other side, proponents of state intervention argued that certain features of the regulatory program—for example, the affirmative requirement to cover issues of public importance—might guard against gray speech. These proponents also insisted upon the need to judge the efficacy of the fairness doctrine or other access regulations on a comparative basis. Even assuming some self-censorship due to regulation, broadcasting might be more varied and more keyed to public issues than if the regulation did not exist at all. To assess fully the impact of access regulations, one must look not simply to the incidents of self-censorship but the whole program of access regulations, and imagine how varied broadcasting or coverage would be if these regulations did not exist. Only then can we know whether they enrich or impoverish public debate.

This objection to access regulations turned on empirical judgments about their likely consequences, but others were more principled. Specifically, some critics argued that access regulations, by their very nature, are not content-neutral, and thus violate the principle prohibiting content regulation. This principle is founded on the idea that the choice over public issues belongs to the public, and that state officials should not determine the merit of ideas or even favor one side over another in a public debate. State officials must be neutral on public issues and let the people decide what is best for themselves. Such a requirement of state neutrality seems attractive, firmly rooted in democratic theory,[29] but I do not see it as barring access regulations either in the United States or in the new democracies of the East.

Admittedly, content judgments are inevitable in access regulations. With program regulation, content judgments are made directly; with structural regulation, indirectly. Given the scarcity of resources and the multiplicity of issues and viewpoints, state officials cannot avoid judgments as to what views or positions to favor, whether they are awarding subsidies, granting preferences to groups in the licensing process, or determining whether an issue is one of public importance. But the purpose of such content judgments is not to determine outcome, but only to protect the integrity of the deliberative process. In fashioning or enforcing access regulations, the state is functioning like a parliamentarian, trying to make certain that the public is fully informed. It is almost as though the state were saying, "We have heard that point several times now," or "Let's hear from the other side."

In making these calls the state *qua* parliamentarian is obviously looking to the content of what is said. However, the rule requiring content neutrality should not bar the state from doing so, for properly understood, that rule bars only those content judgments that have no purpose or justification other than to shape outcome. Of course, any regulation of process will necessarily affect outcome. Yet the choice that democratic theory seeks to insulate from state influence or control is one preceded by full debate, not one that is uninformed or ill-considered. Although a fully informed citizen is likely to make a different decision than an uninformed one, the state's role in educating the citizen and thus producing a different outcome is not at all inconsistent with democratic principles.

Of course, sly politicians can always say they are interested in regulating only process when in fact their sole purpose is to manipulate outcome. The danger of such manipulation calls for institutional arrangements that take program or structural regulation out of the hands of those most intensely interested in political outcomes and place it in the hands of agencies that are relatively removed from politics. In the United States, for example, we placed the administration of the fairness doctrine and control over the licensing process in the hands of the FCC rather than the President or Congress. Similarly, we established an independent public corporation, the Corporation for Public Broadcasting, to administer the congressionally funded radio and television networks. This corporation is still dependent on annual appropriations but otherwise is insulated from direct control by Congress or the President.[30]

These measures built on a long American tradition, dating from the turn of the century, of independent regulatory agencies. Obviously, the emerging democracies of the East have no such tradition on which to rely, and must therefore be especially inventive. They must create new institutions that are part of the state, yet removed from direct political control. The difficulties inherent in such a task, especially where the totalitarian regime of the recent past politicized all institutions, are indeed formidable. Still, this challenge is no more daunting than creating the institutions of advanced capitalism—a banking system or a securities market—out of the shambles of state socialism.

Even with such independent agencies or institutions, the risk still persists that the power to make content judgments will be used, not to preserve the integrity of public debate, but to skew the debate in favor of one outcome. Although the regulators say they want the public to hear both sides of the debate on some proposed tax law, they give access only to the proponents of the law or curb the speech of business interests because they want the measure enacted. The risk of a skewed outcome can be minimized but can never be eliminated altogether. On the other hand, by adopting a strong prophylactic rule—one denying state officials any power whatsoever to make judgments based on content—a government would simply allow the debate to be wholly shaped by the market, which, of course, is not neutral as to content. The biases of the market are not produced by government officials acting deliberately, but rather derive from businesspeople competing with one another. Nevertheless, from democracy's perspective, the concern is just as great. Democracy requires full and open debate on all issues of public importance. Any constraint on that debate threatens democracy, regardless of the identity of the interfering entity or the precise nature of the dynamic that brings it into being.

Access regulations not only require the government to make content judgments, but also sometimes—especially in the case of program regulation—require a newspaper or television or radio station to carry a message or article that the owners of the enterprise find odious. The purpose of such a requirement is not to punish or humble the newspaper or station for having engaged in scandalous reporting, but rather to increase the amount of information and number of viewpoints available to the public. Still, some critics question whether such compulsion is consistent with the guarantee that individuals remain free not to support or affirm an idea that they find offensive. In the United States that principle found expression in a famous Supreme Court decision, *West Virginia Board of Education v. Barnette*;[31] elsewhere, it may be seen as a necessary corollary of democracy.

Decided in 1943, in the midst of war, the *Barnette* decision was a powerful affirmation of freedom of conscience and religious liberty. The Supreme Court refused to capitulate to the patriotic fervor then sweeping the country and protected young schoolchildren from being compelled to salute the American flag. These children, who were Jehovah's Witnesses, found the pledge of allegiance inconsistent with their faith.[32] The Court's decision did not seem to apply to the various regulations of the type I am recommending. In fact, access regulations were never challenged on *Barnette*-type grounds during the period in which they were first developed. However, in the late 1980s the Supreme Court, in *Pacific Gas & Electric Co. v. Public Utilities Commission*,[33] ripped the right not to speak from its original context and used it to invalidate an access regulation developed by the state of California for public utilities, thereby casting serious doubts on the validity of all access regulations.

In the *Pacific Gas* case, a power company challenged a regulation requiring it to allow a public interest organization to use the so-called "extra space" in its monthly billing envelope in order to reach the public. The extra space consisted of the space in a billing envelope that could carry an insert, in addition to the ordinary bill, without increasing the minimum postage charge. The power company had previously used that space for distributing its own newsletter, until the utility commission allocated it to the public interest group to use four times a year. In response, the Supreme Court invoked the *Barnette* principle and concluded that the utility commission had violated the free speech guarantee of the First Amendment.

The significance of *Pacific Gas* for program regulation of the press was immediately recognized. The author of the plurality opinion, Justice Powell, made reference to the earlier Court decision invalidating the Florida right-to-reply statute to support his conclusion, and in 1987 the FCC read *Pacific Gas* as requiring it to abandon the fairness doctrine.[34] If requiring a utility company to carry in its billing envelope a message that it finds offensive violates the First Amendment, the FCC reasoned, requiring a network to broadcast a show that it finds offensive would also violate the First Amendment. In my view, both the Supreme Court's decision in *Pacific Gas* and the FCC's extension of it to the press are questionable.

In a society in which the press is privately owned, program regulation or state-mandated access compromises property rights and diminishes the economic values associated with those rights. The mandated message or program may displace an article or program a station or publisher deems more profitable. The displaced message can only be carried if extra pages are added or the broadcast day is somehow extended. The economic loss may be small, but it is still a loss.

Some may see this economic loss as imposing a duty of compensation on the state, under the constitutional principle—commonplace in capitalist societies—that property cannot be taken for public use without compensation. However, the Supreme Court rejected a claim of compensation in a case involving still another type of access regulation—California required shopping center owners to allow political activists on their property for purposes of reaching the public.[35] The Supreme Court ruled that the economic loss caused by this requirement of the state (protest activities may induce shoppers to stay away) was only a regulation, not a taking of property. In reaching this conclusion, the Court placed great stress on the general application of the regulation.

Wisely, *Pacific Gas* did not question this ruling. No member of the Court thought that the utility commission regulation was a taking of the power company's property. Presumably, the result would be the same in a press case or a case involving a business without a government-conferred monopoly. If the economic loss occasioned by granting access to a shopping center or a billing envelope is not a taking, neither is the economic loss suffered by the press when access to it is granted. Although there is an economic loss, most government regulation of business involves such a loss, and none of the special conditions that transform regulations into takings are present.

The free speech claim does not arise from the economic loss alone, but rather from the compulsion of owners to support financially ideas that they may disagree with or actually detest. It is hard, however, to turn this objection into a viable principle of constitutional law without dismantling the modern democratic state. The entire taxation system is predicated on the idea that money taken from citizens may go to support activities they dislike, like war, parades, particular lectures at state universities, or controversial books in public libraries. Such compelled financial support is an obligation of citizenship, necessary to serve community purposes, which in the case of access regulations include the preservation of the democratic process itself. The reasonable use of an individual's property to support activities he or she detests is a necessary price of democracy.

The Court faintly acknowledged this idea in *Pacific Gas*. Justice Powell readily admitted that the power company could be taxed or assessed for purposes of supporting the public interest group.[36] Given that admission, the objection to directly giving access to the billing envelope to this public interest group is hard to comprehend. There is no functional difference between, on the one hand, giving the public interest group the space ordinarily used by the power company and then requiring the company to pay the extra postage and, on the other hand, taxing or assessing the power company and then giving the money to the public interest group in order to disseminate its ideas. No constitutional difference exists between property and its economic value, or, to put the point more generally, between program and structural regulation.

Of course, giving access to some specific items of property—a shopping center, mailing envelope, newspaper, radio station, or television channel—presents a risk of false attribution not present with taxation. Some readers or viewers might think the message conveyed is that of the publisher or station rather than the view of the person or organization given access. For that reason, the right claimed in *Pacific Gas* is often described as a right against forced association instead of a right not to speak (as in the *Barnette* case). However, as the shopping center case demonstrates, few people would falsely attribute to the utility company, the publisher, or the television station the ideas of those who have been given access. In any event, the danger of false attribution should require a disclaimer, not denial of access altogether. Requiring an organization to issue a disclaimer—for example, "the ideas presented are not those of the station"—forces that organization to speak, but not in the way that the child in *Barnette* was forced to speak. This speech does not perpetuate an orthodoxy; it makes the opposite possible.

Like the rule against content regulation, the rule protecting the right not to speak should not be read as a bar to access regulations. Both rules have an important role to play in democratic societies, but the proper domain of these rules must be carefully delineated. They should not be read as precluding state regulation that broadens public debate and thus enables the press to perform its democratic mission. We in the United States have often overlooked this point, and over the last twenty years have used these two principles to cast access regulations, especially program regulations, into doubt. It can only be hoped that the reconstructive enterprises now afoot in the East will not replicate this experience.

In building a free press, the reformers should look to the American experience, but only selectively. They must create for the press a measure of autonomy from the state without delivering the press totally and completely to the vicissitudes of the market. Privatization of the most rigid and unrelenting variety, denying any role whatsoever for access regulations, may be a step beyond the dictatorships of the past, but it is still a great distance from the dreams of 1989.

Notes

Chapter 1

1. Harry Kalven, Jr., A Worthy Tradition: Freedom of Speech in America (1988).
2. Karl Llewellyn, The Common Law Tradition (1960).
3. T.S. Eliot, *Tradition and the Individual Talent, in* Selected Prose of T.S. Eliot 37 (Frank Kermode ed., 1975) (first published in 1919).
4. Federal Election Campaign Act Amendments of 1974, Pub. L. No. 93-443, 88 Stat. 1263 (codified at 2 U.S.C. §§ 431–437h, 438, 439, 441, 455, 456, 490a, 490b, 490c, 5 U.S.C. §§ 1501–1503, 26 U.S.C. §§ 2766, 6012, 9001–9012, 9031–9042 (1982)).
5. Charles E. Lindblom, Politics and Markets: The World's Political-Economic Systems (1977).
6. *Id.* at 201–21.
7. Miami Herald Publishing Co. v. Tornillo, 418 U.S. 241 (1974).
8. Columbia Broadcasting Sys. v. Democratic Nat'l Comm., 412 U.S. 94 (1973).
9. Buckley v. Valeo, 424 U.S. 1 (1976).
10. First Nat'l Bank of Boston v. Bellotti, 435 U.S. 765 (1978).
11. Lloyd Corp. v. Tanner, 407 U.S. 551 (1972).
12. New York Times Co. v. Sullivan, 376 U.S. 254, 270 (1964).
13. San Antonio Indep. School Dist. v. Rodriguez, 411 U.S. 1 (1973).
14. *But see* Norman Dorsen & Joel Gora, *Free Speech, Property, and the Burger Court: Old Values, New Balances,* 1982 Sup. Ct. Rev. 195.
15. *See, e.g.,* Gerald Gunther, *Learned Hand and the Origins of Modern First Amendment Doctrine: Some Fragments of History,* 27 Stan. L. Rev. 719 (1975); Harry Kalven, Jr., *Professor Ernst Freund and* Debs v. United States, 40 U. Chi. L. Rev. 235 (1973).
16. 395 U.S. 444 (1969).
17. *Id.* at 447–49.
18. *See, e.g.,* Schenck v. United States, 249 U.S. 47 (1919); Froltwerk v. United States, 249 U.S. 204 (1919); Debs v. United States, 249 U.S. 211 (1919).
19. Harry Kalven, Jr., *The New York Times Case: A Note on "The Central Meaning of the First Amendment,"* 1964 Sup. Ct. Rev. 191.
20. *See* Alexander Meiklejohn, *The First Amendment Is an Absolute,* 1961 Sup. Ct. Rev. 245; *see also* William J. Brennan, Jr., *The Supreme Court and the Meiklejohn Interpretation of the First Amendment,* 79 Harv. L. Rev. 1 (1965).
21. *See, e.g.,* Lee C. Bollinger, *Free Speech and Intellectual Values,* 92 Yale L.J. 438 (1983). The breadth of the support is indicated by adherents as diverse as Kalven and Bork. *See* Robert H. Bork, *Neutral Principles and Some First Amendment Problems,* 47 Ind. L.J. 1 (1971).

22. On the two free speech values, see Justice Brennan's remarks in William J. Brennan, Jr., *Address,* 32 RUTGERS L. REV. 173 (1979). For an opinion informed by this perspective, see Richmond Newspapers v. Virginia, 448 U.S. 555, 584–89 (1980) (Brennan, J., concurring in judgment). *See also* Jeffrey M. Blum, *The Divisible First Amendment: A Critical Functionalist Approach to Freedom of Speech and Electoral Campaign Spending,* 58 N.Y.U. L. REV. 1273 (1983).

23. *See, e.g.,* JEROME A. BARRON, FREEDOM OF THE PRESS FOR WHOM? THE RIGHT OF ACCESS TO MASS MEDIA (1973).

24. Herbert Marcuse, *Repressive Tolerance, in* A CRITIQUE OF PURE TOLERANCE 81 (1965).

25. The metaphor stems from Holmes's famous dissent in Abrams v. United States, 250 U.S. 616, 630 (1919) (Holmes, J., dissenting) ("But when men have realized that time has upset many fighting faiths, they may come to believe even more than they believe the very foundations of their own conduct that the ultimate good desired is better reached by free trade in ideas—that the best test of truth is the power of the thought to get itself accepted in the competition of the market . . . . "). The actual phrase "marketplace of ideas" is, oddly enough, Brennan's. *See* Lamont v. Postmaster General, 381 U.S. 301, 308 (1965) (Brennan, J., concurring). The deliberative element in Brennan's thinking about the First Amendment can ultimately be traced to Brandeis, who is often linked to Holmes in his use of the clear and present danger test, but who in fact had no taste for the market metaphor. On the poetics of the tradition, see the inspired essay by David Cole, *Agon at Agora: Creative Misreading in the First Amendment Tradition,* 95 YALE L.J. 857 (1986).

26. *See* Ronald H. Coase, *The Market for Goods and the Market for Ideas,* 64 AM. ECON. REV. PAPERS & PROC. 384 (1974); Aaron Director, *The Parity of the Economic Market Place,* 7 J.L. & ECON. 1 (1964).

27. Red Lion Broadcasting Co. v. FCC, 395 U.S. 367 (1969).

28. Included are Archibald Cox and Herbert Wechsler (the lawyer for the *New York Times* in *New York Times Co. v. Sullivan*). *See* Brief for Respondents Radio Television News Directors Ass'n and Brief for Respondent Columbia Broadcasting System, Red Lion Broadcasting Co. v. FCC, 395 U.S. 367 (1967).

29. HARRY KALVEN, JR., THE NEGRO AND THE FIRST AMENDMENT 140–45 (1965).

30. 340 U.S. 315 (1951).

31. Terminiello v. Chicago, 337 U.S. 1, 37 (1949) (Jackson, J., dissenting) ("[I]f the Court does not temper its doctrinaire logic with a little practical wisdom, it will convert the constitutional Bill of Rights into a suicide pact").

32. *See* Robert B. McKay, *The Preference for Freedom,* 34 N.Y.U. L. REV. 1182 (1959).

33. *See* Owen M. Fiss, *Inappropriateness of the Intent Test in Equal Protection Cases,* 74 F.R.D. 276 (1977) (remarks presented at the Annual Judicial Conference, Second Judicial Circuit of the United States, Sept. 11, 1976).

34. *See* Owen M. Fiss, *Groups and the Equal Protection Clause,* 5 PHIL. & PUB. AFF. 107 (1976).

35. First Nat'l Bank of Boston v. Bellotti, 435 U.S. 765, 809–12 (1978) (White, J., dissenting). The phrase "drown out" appears in the majority opinion, in a paraphrase of the appellee's argument. 435 U.S. at 789 (Powell, J.).

36. PruneYard Shopping Center v. Robins, 447 U.S. 74, 96–101 (1980) (Powell, J., concurring in part and in the judgment).

37. *Id.* at 99.

38. *See, e.g.,* First Nat'l Bank of Boston v. Bellotti, 435 U.S. 765, 790–91 (1978) (quoting Buckley v. Valeo, 424 U.S. 1, 48–49 (1976)).

39. Board of Educ. v. Pico, 457 U.S. 853 (1982).

40. *Id.* at 908–10 (Rehnquist, J., dissenting).

41. Regan v. Taxation with Representation of Washington, 461 U.S. 540 (1983).

42. *See* FCC v. League of Women Voters, 468 U.S. 364, 400–401 (1984).

43. *See* Columbia Broadcasting Sys. v. Democratic Nat'l Comm., 412 U.S. 94, 170–204 (1973) (Brennan, J., dissenting).

Chapter 2

1. *See* Robert L. Rabin, *Federal Regulation in Historical Perspective,* 38 STAN. L. REV. 1189, 1192 (1986).

2. 198 U.S. 45 (1905).

3. 250 U.S. 616, 624 (1919) (Holmes, J., dissenting).

4. *Id.* at 630.

5. *See* Ronald H. Coase, *The Market for Goods and the Market for Ideas,* 64 AM. ECON. REV. PAPERS & PROC. 384 (1974); Aaron Director, *The Parity of the Economic Market Place,* 7 J.L. & ECON. 1 (1964).

6. *See* Owen M. Fiss, *Groups and the Equal Protection Clause,* 5 PHIL. & PUB. AFF. 107, 147 (1976).

7. New York Times Co. v. Sullivan, 376 U.S. 254, 270 (1964).

8. *See* Robert H. Bork, *Neutral Principles and Some First Amendment Problems,* 47 IND. L.J. 1, 26 (1971).

9. *See* FREDERICK SCHAUER, FREE SPEECH: A PHILOSOPHICAL ENQUIRY 11–12 (1982).

10. *See, e.g.,* New York Times Co. v. United States, 403 U.S. 713, 717–18 (1971) (Black, J., concurring).

11. RENATA ADLER, RECKLESS DISREGARD 17 (1986).

12. 347 U.S. 483 (1954); 349 U.S. 294 (1955).

13. *See, e.g.,* Seth F. Kreimer, *Allocational Sanctions: The Problem of Negative Rights in a Positive State,* 132 U. PA. L. REV. 1293, 1297 (1984).

14. *See* LAURENCE GOODWYN, DEMOCRATIC PROMISE: THE POPULIST MOMENT IN AMERICA (1976).

15. *See* CHARLES E. LINDBLOM, POLITICS AND MARKETS: THE WORLD'S POLITICAL-ECONOMIC SYSTEMS 201–21 (1977).

16. *See* Karl E. Klare, *Judicial Deradicalization of the Wagner Act and the Origins of Modern Legal Consciousness, 1937–41,* 62 MINN. L. REV. 265 (1978).

17. 412 U.S. 94 (1973).

18. *See* Letter to Samuel Kercheval (Sept. 5, 1816), *reprinted in* THE POLITICAL WRITINGS OF THOMAS JEFFERSON 97–98 (Edward Dumbauld ed. 1955).

19. *See* HANNAH ARENDT, *What Is Freedom? in* BETWEEN PAST AND FUTURE: EIGHT EXERCISES IN POLITICAL THOUGHT 143, 153 (enlarged ed. 1968). *See generally* HANNAH ARENDT, THE HUMAN CONDITION (1958); HANNAH ARENDT, ON REVOLUTION (1963).

Chapter 3

1. Red Lion Broadcasting Co. v. FCC, 395 U.S. 367 (1969).

2. Miami Herald Publishing Co. v. Tornillo, 418 U.S. 241 (1974); *see also* Pacific Gas Elec. Co. v. Public Util. Comm'n, 475 U.S. 1 (1986) (holding unconstitutional regulation requiring public interest newsletter in billing envelope).

3. Columbia Broadcasting Sys. v. Democratic Nat'l Comm., 412 U.S. 94 (1973).

4. Syracuse Peace Council v. Television Station WTVH, 2 F.C.C.R. 5272 (1987), 3 F.C.C.R. 2035 (1988).

5. Syracuse Peace Council v. FCC, 867 F.2d 654 (D.C. Cir. 1989).

6. CBS v. FCC, 453 U.S. 367 (1981).

7. Metro Broadcasting, Inc. v. FCC, 497 U.S. 547 (1990).

8. Lamprecht v. FCC, 958 F.2d 382 (D.C. Cir. 1992).

9. 308 U.S. 147 (1939).

10. *Id.* at 161.

11. 303 U.S. 444 (1938).

12. *Schneider,* 308 U.S. at 162.

13. *Id.* at 161.

14. HARRY KALVEN, JR., A WORTHY TRADITION: FREEDOM OF SPEECH IN AMERICA 156, 197 (1988).

15. *See, e.g.,* Cox v. Louisiana, 379 U.S. 536, 553–58 (1965) (reversing conviction of speaker for obstruction of sidewalk); Edwards v. South Carolina, 372 U.S. 229, 235–37 (1963) (holding that use of breach of peace ordinance to ban demonstrations violates First Amendment rights of civil rights protesters); *see also* NAACP v. Button, 371 U.S. 415, 428–29 (1963) (holding that Virginia statute banning solicitation of legal business infringes First Amendment rights of NAACP).

16. *See* Harry Kalven, Jr., *The Concept of the Public Forum:* Cox v. Louisiana, 1965 SUP. CT. REV. 1; HARRY KALVEN, JR., THE NEGRO AND THE FIRST AMENDMENT (1965) (republished with the *Public Forum* article in 1966); *see also* Robert C. Post, *Between Governance and Management: The History and Theory of the Public Forum,* in CONSTITUTIONAL DOMAINS: DEMOCRACY, COMMUNITY, MANAGEMENT 199 (1995).

17. 466 U.S. 789 (1984).

18. *See* Heffron v. International Soc'y for Krishna Consciousness, 452 U.S. 640, 649–51 (1981) (employing categorical analysis to review state regulation of solicitation at state fair); United States v. O'Brien, 391 U.S. 367, 376–80 (1968) (using categorical analysis to review a regulation against destroying draft cards).

19. See John Hart Ely, *Flag Desecration: A Case Study in the Roles of Categorization and Balancing in First Amendment Analysis,* 88 HARV. L. REV. 1482, 1500–01 (1975). Professor Ely argued that the Warren Court favored using categorization analysis in First Amendment cases as a way to limit judicial discretion. *See also* Employment Div. v. Smith, 490 U.S. 872 (1990) (Justice Scalia applying categorization analysis to free exercise claims).

20. *Vincent,* 466 U.S. at 795.

21. *Id.* at 804–05.

22. *Id.* at 804.

23. *Id.* at 806.

24. *Id.* at 807.

25. *Vincent,* 466 U.S. at 817, quoting 376 U.S. 254, 270 (1964).

26. *See* United States v. O'Brien, 391 U.S. 367, 377 (1968).

27. *Vincent,* 466 U.S. at 808.

28. *Id.* at 810.

29. Note the word "amongst" in the passage quoted from *Schneider,* 308 U.S. at 162.

30. *Vincent,* 466 U.S. at 812.

31. *Schneider,* 308 U.S. at 163.

32. 497 U.S. 720 (1990).

33. *Id.* at 738–739.

34. *Id.* at 727. Later, Justice O'Connor took up the defendants' argument, based on standard doctrine, that banning solicitation was not the least restrictive means of furthering the Postal Service's interest in becoming more efficient. She immediately cut off such inquiries, however, by disavowing any form of the strict scrutiny or weighted balancing test: "Even if more narrowly tailored regulations could be promulgated, however, the Postal Service is only required to adopt *reasonable* regulations ... . " *Id.* at 735–736.

35. This suggestion is reinforced by the position O'Connor subsequently took in International Soc'y for Krishna Consciousness v. Lee, 112 S. Ct. 2701 (1992), and Lee v. International Soc'y for Krishna Consciousness, 112 S. Ct. 2709 (1992), where she supported a ban on solicitation in the New York area airports, but voted against a ban on airport leafletting. *See* 112 S. Ct. 2711, 2715 (O'Connor, J., concurring); *infra* notes 44 and 47. Justice Kennedy also divided his vote in this way, but, as in *Kokinda,* applied the intermediate standard of review. 112 S. Ct. 2711, 2724 (Kennedy, J., concurring).

36. *See* Amalgamated Food Employees Union v. Logan Valley Plaza, 391 U.S. 308 (1968).

37. *See* Hudgens v. NLRB, 424 U.S. 507 (1976); Lloyd v. Tanner, 407 U.S. 551 (1972). *See generally* Moose Lodge No. 107 v. Irvis, 407 U.S. 163 (1972) (holding that awarding racially discriminatory private club liquor license does not satisfy the Fourteenth Amendment's state action requirement).

38. 418 U.S. 298 (1974).

39. Board of Educ. v. Pico, 457 U.S. 853, 920 (1982) (Rehnquist, J., dissenting); *see* FCC v. League of Women Voters, 468 U.S. 364, 405 (1984) (Rehnquist, J., dissenting); First Nat'l Bank v. Bellotti, 435 U.S. 765, 823–25 (1978) (Rehnquist, J., dissenting). *See also* Regan v. Taxation with Representation, 461 U.S. 540, 544 (1983); Rust v. Sullivan, 500 U.S. 173 (1991).

40. International Soc'y for Krishna Consciousness v. Lee, 112 S. Ct. 2701 (1992).

41. *Id.* at 2724.

42. *Id.* at 2704.

43. *Id.* at 2713.

44. A majority of five justices applied the same lax standard of review to the leafletting regulation of the Port Authority, but only four—Rehnquist, White, Scalia, and Thomas—found it satisfied. O'Connor broke from this group. While she found the lax standard satisfied in the case of the solicitation ban, she concluded that a companion ban on leafletting in the terminals "cannot be upheld as reasonable on this record." 112 S. Ct. at 2713. Justice O'Connor acknowledged the litter rationale of *Schneider* but characterized that only as *a possible* explanation for the regulation. *Id.* at 2714. She repeatedly emphasized, "Here, the Port Authority provided no independent reason for prohibiting leafletting, and the record contains no information from which we can draw an inference that would support its ban." *Id.* Rehnquist and the other three Justices found this position implausible; Rehnquist spoke of the problems of congestion and delay, and virtually invited the Port Authority to return to the Court on the basis of a more complete record. International Soc'y for Krishna Consciousness v. Lee, 112 S. Ct. 2709, 2710.

45. United States v. Kokinda, 497 U.S. 720, 725 (1990).

46. *Id.* at 730 (quoting Perry Educ. Ass'n v. Perry Local Educators Ass'n, 460 U.S. 37, 46 (1983)).

47. The Port Authority case seems to be an exception to this generalization, for in that case, Justice O'Connor, using the lax standard review of *Kokinda*, found the leafletting regulation unconstitutional. *See supra* note 44. Yet no other Justice supported her position, nor is it clear whether this position was based on a strategic failure of the Port Authority— a failure to give a good reason or build the record necessary for the Court to infer one— or whether Justice O'Connor was creating a new tier of scrutiny—lax-plus, lying somewhere between the lax and intermediate standards of review. Perhaps she was having some second thoughts about *Kokinda*, and was suggesting that though the reason for banning leafletting need be neither compelling nor substantial, it has to be a little more than just permissible.

48. *Kokinda,* 497 U.S. at 726.

49. 307 U.S. 496 (1939).

50. See Chapter 5.

51. United States v. Eichman, 496 U.S. 310 (1990); Texas v. Johnson, 491 U.S. 397 (1989).

52. *See* KALVEN, A WORTHY TRADITION, *supra* note 14, at 3–298 (synthesizing and celebrating the Warren Court legacy regarding content regulation).

53. *See, e.g.,* Gertz v. Robert Welch, Inc., 418 U.S. 323, 339 (1974).

54. Hustler Magazine, Inc. v. Falwell, 485 U.S. 46 (1988).

Chapter 4

1. *See generally* ANDREA DWORKIN & CATHARINE A. MACKINNON, PORNOGRAPHY AND CIVIL RIGHTS: A NEW DAY FOR WOMEN'S EQUALITY (1988); CATHARINE A. MACKINNON, ONLY WORDS (1993); CATHARINE A. MACKINNON, TOWARD A FEMINIST THEORY OF THE STATE (1989) [hereinafter MACKINNON, FEMINIST THEORY]; CATHARINE A. MACKINNON, *Francis Biddle's Sister: Pornography, Civil Rights, and Speech, in* FEMINISM UNMODIFIED 163 (1987).

2. *See, e.g,* Alice Echols, *The Taming of the Id: Feminist Sexual Politics, 1968–83, in* PLEASURE AND DANGER 50 (Carole S. Vance ed., 1984); Ellen Willis, *Feminism, Moralism, and Pornography, in* POWERS OF DESIRE: THE POLITICS OF SEXUALITY 460 (Ann Snitow et al. eds., 1983). *See also* Nan D. Hunter & Sylvia A. Law, Brief Amici Curiae of Feminist Anti-Censorship Taskforce et al., American Booksellers Ass'n v. Hudnut, 21 U. MICH. J.L. REF. 69 (1987).

3. American Booksellers Ass'n v. Hudnut, 771 F.2d 323 (7th Cir. 1985), *aff'd per curiam,* 475 U.S. 1001 (1986).

4. *See, e.g.,* MACKINNON, ONLY WORDS, *supra* note 1, at 91–97.

5. Section 16-15 makes unlawful those discriminatory practices listed in § 16-3(g), including these pornography-related offenses:

> (4) Trafficking in pornography: The production, sale, exhibition, or distribution of pornography . . . .
> (5) Coercion into a pornographic performance: Coercing, intimidating or fraudulently inducing any person, including a man [or] transsexual, into performing for pornography, which injury may date from any appearance or sale of any products of such performance . . . .

(6) Forcing pornography on a person: The forcing of pornography on any woman, man, child, or transsexual in any place of employment, in education, in a home, or in any public place.

(7) Assault or physical attack due to pornography: The assault, physical attack, or injury of any woman, man, child, or transsexual in a way that is directly caused by specific pornography.

Indianapolis and Marion County, Ind., City-County General Ordinance No. 35 § 1, § 16-3 (June 4, 1984) [hereinafter Indianapolis Ordinance]. Section 16-26(d) allows the equal opportunity advisory board to issue cease-and-desist orders against anyone found to be engaging in an unlawful discriminatory practice and to award damages to victims of discriminatory practices that violate the Code. The full text of the ordinance can be found in DWORKIN & MACKINNON, *supra* note 1, at 106.

6. Indianapolis Ordinance, *supra* note 5, § 8.

7. Central to this provision is the life story of Linda Marchiano, who under the stage name Linda Lovelace starred in the famous pornographic movie *Deep Throat.* LINDA LOVELACE WITH MIKE MCGRADY, ORDEAL (1980). *See also* MACKINNON, *Linda's Life and Andrea's Work, in* FEMINISM UNMODIFIED, *supra* note 1, at 127–33 (1987).

8. *Cf.* Grosjean v. American Press Co., 297 U.S. 233 (1936).

9. *See* Schneider v. State, 308 U.S. 147, 162 (1939) (holding that municipal ordinance prohibiting distribution of printed matter in order to keep streets clean violates the First Amendment). For more recent developments, see Chapter 3, "Silence on the Street Corner."

10. The ordinance made a gesture in this direction by providing that, in the context of "coerced performances":

(A) Proof of the following facts or conditions shall not constitute a defense:
I. That the person is a woman; or
II. That the person is or has been a prostitute; or
III. That the person has attained the age of majority; or
IV. That the person is connected by blood or marriage to anyone involved in or related to the making of the pornography; or
V. That the person has previously had, or been thought to have had, sexual relations with anyone, including anyone involved in or related to the making of the pornography; or
VI. That the person has previously posed for sexually explicit pictures for or with anyone, including anyone involved in or related to the making of the pornography at issue; or
VII. That anyone else, including a spouse or other relative, has given permission on the person's behalf; or
VIII. That the person actually consented to a use of the performance that is changed into pornography; or
IX. That the person knew that the purpose of the acts or events in question was to make pornography; or
X. That the person demonstrated no resistance or appeared to cooperate actively in the photographic sessions or in the sexual events that produced the pornography; or
XI. That the person signed a contract, or made statements affirming a willingness to cooperate in the production of pornography; or
XII. That no physical force, threats, or weapons were used in the making of the pornography; or
XIII. That the person was paid or otherwise compensated.

Indianapolis Ordinance, *supra* note 5, §§ 1, 16-3(g)(5).

11. American Booksellers Ass'n v. Hudnut, 771 F.2d 323, 332–33 (7th Cir. 1985), *aff'd per curiam,* 475 U.S. 1001 (1986).

12. *See* New York Times v. Sullivan, 376 U.S. 254, 279 (1964) (critics of government would be deterred by a rule allowing libel judgments for any false statement).

13. *Id.* at 273.

14. *Id.* at 279–80.

15. Indianapolis Ordinance, *supra* note 5, §§ 1, 16-3(g)(7)–(8).

16. *American Booksellers Ass'n,* 771 F.2d at 325.

17. *See infra* note 22 (statutory definition of pornography).

18. *American Booksellers Ass'n,* 771 F.2d at 325.

19. *See, e.g,* DWORKIN & MACKINNON, *supra* note 1, at 15–16, 24–30 (sexism is more pervasive than other forms of discrimination because pornography has, throughout history, consistently defined women in unequal roles); MACKINNON, *Francis Biddle's Sister, supra* note 1, at 163–97 (same); PORNOGRAPHY: RESEARCH ADVANCES AND POLICY CONSIDERATIONS (Dolf Zillmann & Jennings Bryant eds., 1989).

20. *See, e.g.,* Police Dep't of Chicago v. Mosley, 408 U.S. 92, 95–96 (1972) (invalidating Chicago ordinance that barred all pickets near schools except those by organized labor, on the ground that the city had no compelling interest in favoring labor pickets).

21. The Indianapolis City Council found that:

Pornography is a discriminatory practice based on sex which denies women equal opportunities in society. Pornography is central in creating and maintaining sex as a basis for discrimination. Pornography is a systematic practice of exploitation and subordination based on sex which differentially harms women. The bigotry and contempt it promotes, with the acts of aggression it fosters, harm women's opportunities for equality of rights in employment, education, access to and use of public accommodations, and acquisition of real property; promote rape, battery, child abuse, kidnapping and prostitution and inhibit just enforcement of laws against such acts; and contribute significantly to restricting women in particular from full exercise of citizenship and participation in public life, including in neighborhoods.

Indianapolis Ordinance, *supra* note 5, §§ 1, 16-1(a)(2).

22. The full definition reads:

Pornography shall mean the graphic sexually explicit subordination of women, whether in pictures or in words, that also includes one or more of the following:

(1) Women are presented as sexual objects who enjoy pain or humiliation; or

(2) Women are presented as sexual objects who experience sexual pleasure in being raped; or

(3) Women are presented as sexual objects tied up or cut up or mutilated or bruised or physically hurt, or as dismembered or truncated or fragmented or severed into body parts; or

(4) Women are presented being penetrated by objects or animals; or

(5) Women are presented in scenarios of degradation, injury, abusement, torture, shown as filthy or inferior, bleeding, bruised, or hurt in a context that makes these conditions sexual; and

(6) Women are presented as sexual objects for domination, conquest, violation, exploitation, possession, or use, or through postures or positions of servility or submission or display.

Indianapolis Ordinance, *supra* note 5, §§ 1, 16-3(q).

23. *Id.*

24. *Id.*

25. *Id.*

26. *See* MACKINNON, *Francis Biddle's Sister, supra* note 1, at 172 ("What pornography *does* goes beyond its content: it eroticizes hierarchy, it sexualizes inequality. . . . It institutionalizes the sexuality of male supremacy. . . ."); *see also* ANDREA DWORKIN, PORNOGRAPHY: MEN POSSESSING WOMEN 241 (1981) (pornography's main theme is male power over women).

27. *See generally* Steven G. Gey, *The Apologetics of Suppression: The Regulation of Pornography as Act and Idea,* 86 MICH. L. REV. 1564, 1606–07 (1988).

28. 413 U.S. 15 (1973).

29. *Id.* at 24.

30. A Book Named "John Cleland's Memoirs of a Woman of Pleasure" v. Massachusetts, 383 U.S. 413 (1966).

31. Roth v. United States, 354 U.S. 476, 487–89 (1957).

32. *See, e.g.,* A Book Named "John Cleland's Memoirs of a Woman of Pleasure," 383 U.S. at 420–21 (holding that sale of book with some social value is not constitutionally protected where seller's emphasis is solely on book's sexual content); Mishkin v. New York, 383 U.S. 502 (1966) (holding that prurient-appeal requirement of prevailing obscenity test should be assessed with regard to interests of intended audience).

33. On the history of this branch of American law, see HARRY KALVEN, JR., A WORTHY TRADITION: FREEDOM OF SPEECH IN AMERICA 33–53 (1988) (reviewing evolution of obscenity jurisprudence).

34. *See* Ginsberg v. New York, 390 U.S. 629, 636–38 (1968) (holding that judgment of whether material directed to minors is pornography should be based on its appeal to prurient interests of juveniles, not adults); New York v. Ferber, 458 U.S. 747, 756 (1982) (holding the *Miller* test need not be satisfied for sexual materials depicting children).

35. Federal Communications Comm'n v. Pacifica Found., 438 U.S. 726, 748–50 (1978) (noting that broadcasting receives "the most limited First Amendment protection" because of its pervasiveness and accessibility to children).

36. *American Booksellers Ass'n,* 771 F.2d at 332.

37. *See* Frederick Schauer, *Causation Theory and the Causes of Sexual Violence,* 1987 AM. B. FOUND. RES. J. 737, 768.

38. R.A.V. v. City of St. Paul, 112 S. Ct. 2538 (1992).

39. *Id.* at 2543.

40. *Id.*

41. *Id.* at 2545 (quoting Simon & Schuster, Inc. v. Members of N.Y. State Crime Victims Bd., 502 U.S. 105, 116 (1991)).

42. "When the basis for the content discrimination consists entirely of the very reason the entire class of speech at issue is proscribable, no significant danger of idea or viewpoint discrimination exists." *R.A.V.,* 112 S. Ct. at 2545.

43. *Id.* at 2546.

44. The coerced performance, forced viewing, and physical assault provisions are selective regulations that involve content discrimination, but the content discrimination is not extraneous. In any event these provisions clearly fall within a number of the exceptions Scalia created to his rule. One exception allows the state to accord differential treatment to a content-defined subcategory of proscribable speech if the subcategory is associated with the so-called "secondary effects" of speech; as he indicated, "A State could, for example, permit all obscene live performances except those involving minors." *Id.* at 2546. A second exception,

crafted with an eye toward Title VII sexual harassment claims, allows the state to make content-based distinctions in cases where the law is "directed not against speech but against conduct" and the speech is "swept up incidentally" as part of the regulatory scheme. *Id.*

45. *See* ALEXANDER MEIKLEJOHN, POLITICAL FREEDOM: THE CONSTITUTIONAL POWERS OF THE PEOPLE 27 (1948) (First Amendment protects discussion of different views as a principle of self-government); Alexander Meiklejohn, *The First Amendment Is an Absolute,* 1961 SUP. CT. REV. 245, 255 (First Amendment protects thoughts and actions necessary for governance).

46. Meiklejohn, *The First Amendment Is an Absolute, supra* note 45, at 263 (quoting Harry Kalven, Jr., *Metaphysics of the Law of Obscenity,* 1960 SUP. CT. REV. 1, 16).

47. Robert H. Bork, *Neutral Principles and Some First Amendment Problems,* 47 IND. L.J. 1 (1971).

48. Gertz v. Robert Welch, Inc., 418 U.S. 323, 339 (1974).

49. *See, e.g.,* Brandenburg v. Ohio, 395 U.S. 444, 447 (1969) (the suppression of the advocacy of force is constitutional only when such advocacy has become an incitement to imminent lawless action); *see also* KALVEN, *supra* note 33, at 119–236 (outlining development of First Amendment exception for incitement).

50. *See* MACKINNON, *Francis Biddle's Sister, supra* note 1, at 193 (pornography silences all women by destroying credibility and devalidating); CATHARINE A. MACKINNON, *The Sexual Politics of the First Amendment, in* FEMINISM UNMODIFIED 206, 208–09 (1987) (First Amendment absolutism protects pornography, "that speech of men that silences the speech of women"). This essay is Professor MacKinnon's response to Judge Easterbrook's opinion. For further elaboration of the silencing theory, see Frank I. Michelman, *Conceptions of Democracy in American Constitutional Argument: The Case of Pornography Regulation,* 56 TENN. L. REV. 291 (1989). For a brief response, see Ronald Dworkin, *Two Concepts of Liberty, in* ISAIAH BERLIN: A CELEBRATION 100, 108–09 (Edna & Avishai Margalit eds., 1991).

51. MACKINNON, *Francis Biddle's Sister, supra* note 1, at 193. A particular variety of this harm arises to the extent that the materials covered by the trafficking offense present rape, mutilation, and battering as sexually arousing entertainment and thus trivialize such acts of violence in the eyes of those (men) in charge of the legislative and administrative machinery of the state.

52. *See* Michelman, *Conceptions of Democracy in American Constitutional Argument, supra* note 50, at 307.

53. Chief Justice Warren himself objected to this practice in Jacobellis v. Ohio, 378 U.S. 184, 202 (1964) (Warren, C.J., dissenting) (arguing that the "Court [should] not establish itself as an ultimate censor," passing independent judgment on each new set of facts). On the so-called "technical preferred position" of the First Amendment, see KALVEN, *supra* note 33, at xxvii.

54. United States v. Dennis, 183 F.2d 201, 212 (2d Cir. 1950) ("In each case [the courts] must ask whether the gravity of the 'evil,' discounted by its improbability, justifies such invasion of free speech as is necessary to avoid the danger"), *aff'd,* 341 U.S. 494 (1951).

Chapter 5

1. The term "X, Y, Z Series" refers to a group of three portfolios. Each portfolio consisted of thirteen photographs; each photograph measured 13 1/2 inches square. The X

Portfolio included scenes that may be considered sadomasochistic, the Y Portfolio consisted of flowers, and the Z Portfolio consisted of photographs of black men. When I viewed the show in the fall of 1989 at the Wadsworth Athenaeum in Hartford, all three portfolios were mounted on a wall at the end of the exhibition. In some other locations, the X Portfolio was displayed horizontally in a glass case, so that museum visitors who passed through the exhibit looking only at the walls would not see it.

2. The prosecution in fact charged the museum and its director with depicting minors in a state of nudity as well as with pandering obscenity. The prosecution singled out seven photographs as the basis for its case: the two of the children and five from the X, Y, Z Series. In one of the five from the X, Y, Z Series, a man is urinating into another man's mouth, another shows the tip of a finger inserted into a penis, and the other three each depict a man with an object inserted in his rectum: a bull whip, a cylinder, and a hand. Presumably, the cylindrical object was a dildo, and the hand was clenched in the form of a fist. The catalog of the exhibition, JANET KARDON, ROBERT MAPPLETHORPE: THE PERFECT MOMENT (1988), does not contain reproductions of all the photographs in the show, and specifically does not include any from the X, Y, Z Series that were targeted by the Cincinnati prosecutor.

3. 354 U.S. 476, 484–85 (1957).

4. A Book Named "John Cleland's Memoirs of a Woman of Pleasure" v. Massachusetts, 383 U.S. 413 (1966).

5. 413 U.S. 15 (1973).

6. Prurient interest of whom? While the Court in *Miller* spoke of the "average person," it included "normal or perverted" sexual acts in its examples of what depictions state obscenity laws permissibly could reach, and on other occasions the Court adjusted the standard to take account of the fact that the allegedly obscene material was aimed at a so-called "deviant audience." Pinkus v. United States, 436 U.S. 293, 301–03 (1978); Ward v. Illinois, 431 U.S. 767, 773 (1977); Mishkin v. New York, 383 U.S. 502, 508–10 (1966).

7. The Cincinnati prosecutor's strategy of singling out the two photographs of the children might be explained by the presence of a statute specifically addressed to the display of minors in a state of nudity. But the decision to single out the five other photographs, contrary to the requirement that the work—here, the exhibition or, at the very least, the X, Y, Z, Series—be taken as a whole has led me to wonder whether the prosecutor was trying to sabotage his own case. This speculation is strengthened by the weakness of the prosecutor's case. The prosecution had only four witnesses testify. Three were policemen who confirmed that the exhibition had taken place. The fourth was a so-called communications expert who, according to the *New York Times,* "worked with anti-pornography groups and whose primary artistic credential was presented as writing songs for the 'Captain Kangaroo' television show." *Obscenity Jurors Were Pulled 2 Ways,* N.Y. TIMES, Oct. 10, 1990, at A12, col. 4.

8. For an understanding of the political dimensions of Mapplethorpe's work, see Ingrid Sischy, *White and Black,* NEW YORKER, Nov. 13, 1989, at 124 (review of shows by Minor White and Robert Mapplethorpe); Amy Adler, The Tragedy of Contemporary Art in America (May 1990) (paper on file with author).

9. *Senate Passes Compromise on Arts Endowment,* N.Y. TIMES, Oct. 25, 1990, at C19, col. 1. The naked man referred to by Senator Helms is actually Robert Mapplethorpe. The photograph is entitled "Self-Portrait, 1978."

10. Act of Oct. 23, 1989, Pub. L. No. 101–121, tit. II, 103 Stat. 701, 738.

11. 135 CONG. REC. S8807–08 (daily ed. July 26, 1989) (statement of Sen. Helms).

12. Act of Oct. 23, 1989, Pub. L. No. 101–121, tit. II, 103 Stat. 701, 738. Particularized sanctions like these were also applied by the 1989 statute to the Southeastern Center for Contemporary Art in South Carolina, which had supported another work—a photograph of a crucifix in urine by Andres Serrano—that angered members of Congress.

13. *Id.* at § 304(a), 103 Stat. at 741.

14. Senator Helms originally proposed the following amendment:

None of the funds authorized to be appropriated pursuant to this Act may be used to promote, disseminate or produce—

(1) obscene or indecent materials, including but not limited to, depictions of sado-masochism, homoeroticism, the exploitation of children, or individuals engaged in sex acts; or

(2) material which denigrates the objects or beliefs of the adherents of a particular religion or non-religion; or

(3) material which denigrates, debases, or reviles a person, group, or class of citizens on the basis of race, creed, sex, handicap, age, or national origin.

H.R. 2788, 101st Cong., 1st Sess., 135 CONG. REC. S8806 (daily ed. July 26, 1989).

15. Arts, Humanities, and Museum Amendments of 1990, Pub. L. No. 101-512, § 103(b), 104 Stat. 1915, 1963 (1990).

16. *Id.* at § 103(h), 104 Stat. at 1965–66.

17. *See* INDEPENDENT COMMISSION, REPORT TO CONGRESS ON THE NATIONAL ENDOWMENT FOR THE ARTS 26 (Sept. 1990).

18. Arts, Humanities, and Museum Amendments of 1990, Pub. L. No. 101-512, § 106(c)(4), 104 Stat. 1915, 1968. The 1990 statute continues the prior procedure for reviewing grants, in which peer-review panels in each artistic discipline recommend applications for funding to the National Council on the Arts (a presidentially appointed advisory body within the NEA), and the Council in turn recommends applications for funding to the chairperson. The 1990 statute gives the chairperson unambiguous power to veto these recommendations, but he or she may not elect to fund an application rejected by the Council.

19. *See* INDEPENDENT COMMISSION, *supra* note 17. The Independent Commission was established by Congress, and its members were appointed by President Bush. Act of Oct. 23, 1989, Pub. L. No. 101-121, § 304(c), 103 Stat. 701, 742.

20. Arts, Humanities, and Museum Amendments of 1990, Pub. L. No. 101-512, § 103(b), 104 Stat. 1915, 1963.

21. Shortly after the adoption of the Helms amendment, the chairperson of the NEA, John Frohnmayer, promulgated a rule that required all NEA recipients to sign a pledge stating that they would comply with the Helms amendment. *See Grants Rule Testimony by Arts Chief,* N.Y. TIMES, May 2, 1990, at C13, col. 1. These pledges caused a furor even greater than the Helms amendment itself, and the National Council on the Arts recommended that the requirement of signing a pledge be dropped. Frohnmayer refused to do so. Moreover, where the NEA had made contributions to the general operating budgets of organizations, like collectives or galleries, that were suspected of having run afoul of the Helms amendment, the NEA demanded the names of every artist the organization supported and a description of every work it planned to exhibit. These measures were foreshadowed by an action Frohnmayer took in November 1989, less than a month after he assumed office, when he rescinded funding for an exhibition about AIDS entitled

"Witnesses: Against Our Vanishing" on the grounds that it was too "political." In justifying this action he pointed to an artist's essay in the catalogue severely criticizing, among others, New York City Cardinal John O'Connor and Senator Helms for their positions on homosexuality and AIDS issues. As Frohnmayer then put it, "I strongly believe in the ability of people to speak their minds under the First Amendment, but the endowment should not be funding that discourse." *Front Page: NEA Chairman Does Turnabout on AIDS Exhibition,* ART IN AMERICA, Jan. 1990, at 31. Frohnmayer reversed his decision within two weeks, but restricted grant funds from being used for the catalogue. *Arts Endowment Withdraws Grant for AIDS Show,* N.Y. TIMES, Nov. 9, 1989, at A1, col. 1; *National Arts Chief, in a Reversal, Gives Grant to AIDS Show,* N.Y. TIMES, Nov. 17, 1989, at A1, col. 1; *Frohnmayer's Folly,* NEW ART EXAMINER, Feb. 1990, at 20. For an analysis of the administration of the NEA under the Helms amendment, and a sense of what the 1990 statute is likely to bring, *see generally* Brian Wallis, *Bush's Compromise: A Newer Form of Censorship?* ART IN AMERICA, Nov. 1990, at 57. The pledge requirement resulted in a number of lawsuits which were brought by organizations whose fiscal year 1990 grants were withheld because they refused to sign the pledge. One such suit was resolved in January 1991 when the federal district court in Los Angeles held the pledge requirement unconstitutionally vague. Bella Lewitsky Dance Found. v. Frohnmayer, 1991 U.S. Dist. Lexis 332, No. 90-3616 (C.D. Cal. Jan. 9, 1991). A second suit, brought by the New School for Social Research in New York, was settled the next month, when the NEA agreed to abandon the pledge requirement for all fiscal year 1990 recipients. *Arts Agency Voids Pledge on Obscenity,* N.Y. TIMES, Feb. 21, 1991, at C14, col. 6. However, a provision in the 1990 statute might be read as giving rise to an analogous requirement insofar as it requires applicants for NEA funds to provide "an assurance that the project . . . will meet the standards of artistic excellence and artistic merit required by this Act." Arts, Humanities, and Museum Amendments of 1990, Pub. L. No. 101-512 § 103(g), 104 Stat. 1915, 1964–65 (1990). The statute goes on to require that grant payments in most cases be made in installments, with the final one-third withheld until "the Chairperson finds that the recipient of such assistance is complying substantially . . . with the conditions under which such assistance is provided to such recipient." *Id.*

22. HARRY KALVEN, JR., A WORTHY TRADITION: FREEDOM OF SPEECH IN AMERICA 301–03 (1988). Kalven distinguishes the criminal sanction (referred to as the direct or total sanction) from partial sanctions on the grounds of motivation:

> The criminal sanction is not ambiguous as to the objective of the state. Its purpose is to prevent the publishing of the disfavored message; it has no other purpose than to dissuade the speaker from saying *that*. In contrast, there is another set of situations in which only a privilege of some sort is at stake, and the state objective—and motivation—may be highly ambiguous.

Id. at 301. But this distinction appears to rest on a mischaracterization, or perhaps an incomplete description, of the purposes of the state. In the criminal context, the state prosecution might threaten to suppress the speech, as Kalven asserts, but its purpose or motivation is much more complex and indeed is not dissimilar from, or less ambiguous than in, the subsidy context. For example, it could be said that the purpose or motive of an obscenity prosecution is not to suppress speech; rather, the purpose might be to preserve or protect norms regarding sexuality or morality, or to prevent rape or other sexual violence, which in turn might require suppression of speech.

23. Recent feminist attacks on pornography—analyzed in Chapter 4—see the free circulation of publications that treat women as sex objects as partially responsible for the silencing of women. *See generally* CATHARINE MACKINNON, FEMINISM UNMODIFIED 127–213 (1987). Speech itself, rather than the act of the state, is responsible for the silencing effect, but under a theory that makes state inaction a form of action, responsibility can be traced to the state through the decision not to prosecute. While I find myself sympathetic to much in this line of argument, it does not dissolve the distinction between the allocative and criminal contexts. The same silencing effect that is decried by feminists may be present when a grant is awarded, so a grant to some artists could be said to have two silencing effects—one linked to the denial of a grant to someone else, and another that flows from the free circulation of the subsidized material.

24. *Compare, e.g.,* Gaston County v. United States, 395 U.S. 285 (1969); Griggs v. Duke Power Co., 401 U.S. 424 (1971); Swann v. Charlotte-Mecklenburg Bd. of Educ., 402 U.S. 1 (1971) *and* Keyes v. School Dist. No. 1, 413 U.S. 189 (1973) *with* Washington v. Davis, 426 U.S. 229 (1976); Village of Arlington Heights v. Metropolitan Hous. Dev. Corp., 429 U.S. 252 (1977); Personnel Adm'r v. Feeney, 442 U.S. 256 (1979) *and* Wards Cove Packing Co. v. Atonio, 490 U.S. 642 (1989). Sometimes the Court casts this procedural approach in terms of "motive" or "intent" rather than "criterion" or "basis." For an analysis of this shift in the school context, see my statement to the *Second Circuit's Annual Judicial Conference,* 74 F.R.D. 219, 276 (1976); and my article, *School Desegregation: The Uncertain Path of the Law,* 4 PHIL. & PUB. AFF. 3 (1974).

25. Board of Educ. v. Pico, 457 U.S. 853 (1982). In this case, Justice Brennan, speaking only for a plurality of the Justices, wrote: "If petitioners *intended* by their removal decision to deny respondents access to ideas with which petitioners disagreed, and if this intent was the decisive factor in petitioners' decision, then petitioners have exercised their discretion in violation of the Constitution." *Id.* at 871 (footnote omitted). He went on to identify a permissible criterion: "On the other hand, respondents implicitly concede that an unconstitutional motivation would *not* be demonstrated if it were shown that petitioners had decided to remove the books at issue because those books were pervasively vulgar." *Id.* As a general matter, Justice Brennan's approach to the First Amendment, like the one advanced in this piece, can be understood as premised on the desire to protect the access of the public to controversial ideas and to avoid the pall of orthodoxy. The emphasis in *Pico* upon the criterion of decision is inconsistent with such an approach, as Justice Rehnquist pointed out in dissent. *Id.* at 915–18. Justice Rehnquist would allow the state a free hand in awarding grants, except when it was shown that the decision was "primarily 'aimed at the suppression of dangerous ideas.'" FCC v. League of Women Voters, 468 U.S. 364, 407 (1984) (Rehnquist, J., dissenting) (quoting, *inter alia,* American Communications Ass'n v. Douds, 339 U.S. 382, 402 (1950)). Later, in Rust v. Sullivan, 500 U.S. 173 (1991), Rehnquist obtained a majority for his position in upholding regulations barring appropriations of federal funds for family planning services offering abortion counseling, referral, and advocacy.

26. *See* Owen M. Fiss, *Groups and The Equal Protection Clause,* 5 PHIL. & PUB. AFF. 107 (1976).

27. Chapters 1 and 2 address the various theories of the First Amendment, and the argument in favor of viewing the First Amendment more as a protection of collective self-determination than of individual self-expression. For a consideration of these issues that postdated those chapters, and that appeared contemporaneously with this one, see Paul

Stern's brilliant Note, *A Pluralistic Reading of the First Amendment and Its Relation to Public Discourse,* 99 YALE L.J. 925 (1990).

28. *Pico,* 457 U.S. at 917 (Rehnquist, J., dissenting).

29. New York Times Co. v. Sullivan, 376 U.S. 254, 270 (1964).

30. The use of certain meritocratic criteria in a way that effectuates a delegation of power over funding decisions to the artistic community might—given certain background assumptions about the nature of that community—produce the desired effect: robust public debate. Under this scheme, effect remains the touchstone of the constitutional wrong, and a criterion approach is deployed for instrumental reasons, to be abandoned whenever it fails to produce the desired effects.

31. *See* Griggs v. Duke Power Co., 401 U.S. 424 (1971); Owen M. Fiss, *A Theory of Fair Employment Laws,* 38 U. CHI. L. REV. 235 (1971); Owen M. Fiss, Gaston County v. United States: *Fruition of the Freezing Principle,* 1969 SUP. CT. REV. 379; Note, *Reading the Mind of the School Board: Segregative Intent and the De Facto/De Jure Distinction,* 86 YALE L.J. 317 (1976).

32. As one of the experts called by the defense in the Cincinnati trial put it, when questioned about some of the sadomasochistic photographs in the X, Y, Z Series, "It's the tension between the physical beauty of the photograph and the brutal nature of what's going on in it that gives it the particular quality that this work of art has." Andy Grundberg, *Critics Notebook: Cincinnati Trial's Unanswered Question,* N.Y. TIMES, Oct. 18, 1990, at C17, col. 3 (quoting Jacquelynn Bass, Director, University Art Museum in Berkeley, California).

33. *See* H.R. 209, 104th Cong., 1st Sess. (1995); 135 CONG. REC. H3637 (daily ed. July 12, 1989) (statement of Rep. Rohrabacher); William Safire, *Stop Subsidizing the Arts,* N.Y. TIMES, May 18, 1990, at A31, col. 6; Robert Pear, *A Hostile House Trains Its Sights on Funds for the Arts,* N.Y. TIMES, January 9, 1995, at A1, col. 6.

34. See Chapter 1, section III, and KALVEN, *supra* note 22, at 89–91, 97–100. *See also* Chapters 4 and 6, discussing two situations—pornography and hate speech—in which failure of government to act might be a form of action.

35. *See* Griffin v. County School Bd., 377 U.S. 218 (1964); Lee v. Macon County Bd. of Educ., 231 F. Supp. 743 (M.D. Ala. 1964); *see also* United States v. Plaquemines Parish School Bd., 291 F. Supp. 841 (E.D. La. 1967) (school board may not reduce funding for newly integrated schools to encourage white flight to private, segregated schools).

36. *See, e.g.,* INDEPENDENT COMMISSION, *supra* note 17, at 85 (Legal Task Force's consensus statement that "there is no constitutional obligation on the part of the federal government to fund the arts").

37. Missouri v. Jenkins, 495 U.S. 33 (1990).

38. As a corollary, it is sometimes argued that a grant or government subsidy constitutes an endorsement or approval of the subsidized work or its message—as though government or individual taxpayers are speaking. Senator Helms took this argument to a new extreme when he reacted to the jury verdict in Cincinnati. "A Helms aide explained," according to the *New York Times,* "that the Senator believed the NEA grant . . . had in effect transformed the photographs into Government-approved art, making it impossible for a jury to declare them obscene." *Cincinnati Jury Acquits Museum in Mapplethorpe Obscenity Case,* N.Y. TIMES, Oct. 6, 1990, at A1, col. 1. To reassure Senator Helms on this point, the 1990 statute specifies that "[t]he disapproval or approval of an application by the Chairperson shall not be construed to mean, and shall not be considered as evidence that [the art funded

by the grant] is or is not obscene." Arts, Humanities, and Museum Amendments of 1990, Pub. L. No. 101-512, § 103(b), 104 Stat. 1915, 1963–64 (1990). In my view, the danger of attribution or endorsement that Helms fears is small, especially when the NEA decision responds to the requirements of the law (a court order or the Constitution). No one will assume that the Mapplethorpe show expresses the viewpoint of the NEA on some particular issue (sadomasochism or homosexuality), or even less, of individual taxpayers who might be offended by the work. In any event, a simple disclaimer can avoid that danger. On the other hand, a decision by the NEA to fund a project ideally would represent some judgment from the agency, subject to judicial review, about the issues that should be considered by the public and the range of views that should be heard, or that are missing from the public debate. These judgments are analogous to the ones made by the state in public education and public broadcasting; far from being denied to the state by the First Amendment, they seek to vindicate its highest purposes.

Chapter 6

1. 112 S. Ct. 2538 (1992).

2. St. Paul, Minn., Legis. Code § 292.02 (1990).

3. *See, e.g.,* New York Times Co. v. United States, 403 U.S. 713, 714–20 (1971) (Black, J., concurring); Hugo L. Black, *The Bill of Rights,* 35 N.Y.U. L. Rev. 865 (1960).

4. 198 U.S. 45 (1905).

5. *See* Tinsley E. Yarbrough, Mr. Justice Black and His Critics 50–51 (1988). For two of the more passionate formulations of this view, see Griswold v. Connecticut, 381 U.S. 479, 513 (1965) (Black, J., dissenting) and Goldberg v. Kelly, 397 U.S. 254, 276–77 (1970) (Black, J., dissenting).

6. *See* Alexander Meiklejohn, *The First Amendment Is an Absolute,* 1961 Sup. Ct. Rev. 245, 255.

7. Chaplinsky v. New Hampshire, 315 U.S. 568 (1942).

8. 112 S. Ct. at 2548. Scalia also objected to the subject covered in that it dealt with racial antagonisms, but not, for example, with animosity addressed to organized labor. That objection is more akin to the partiality present in Police Dep't of Chicago v. Mosley, 408 U.S. 92 (1972), which held a ban on picketing unconstitutional because it exempted labor picketing from its coverage, but seems less central to his decision and to First Amendment principles.

9. *See, e.g.,* Cass R. Sunstein, Democracy and the Problem of Free Speech 193 (1993). Professor Akhil Amar faults the Court for ignoring the Civil War Amendments, principally using the Thirteenth as the source of the equality value, but stops short of accusing the Court of having erred in its choice of values. Akhil R. Amar, *The Case of the Missing Amendments:* R.A.V. v. City of St. Paul, 106 Harv. L. Rev. 124, 151–61 (1992).

10. *See* Noto v. United States, 367 U.S. 290 (1961); Scales v. United States, 367 U.S. 203 (1961); Yates v. United States, 354 U.S. 298 (1957). For a general discussion of these cases, see Harry Kalven, Jr., A Worthy Tradition: Freedom Of Speech in America 211–26 (1988). *See also* Brandenburg v. Ohio, 395 U.S. 444, 447 (1969) (allowing proscriptions against advocating force only when advocacy has become an incitement to imminent lawless action).

11. This formulation was used by Edmond Cahn during the McCarthy period. Edmond Cahn, *The Firstness of the First Amendment,* 65 Yale L.J. 464 (1956). During that same

period some spoke of the First Amendment as a "preferred freedom." *See* Robert B. McKay, *The Preference for Freedom,* 34 N.Y.U. L. REV. 1182 (1959).

12. *See* ALEXANDER MEIKLEJOHN, POLITICAL FREEDOM: THE CONSTITUTIONAL POWERS OF THE PEOPLE 24–28 (1965); Harry Kalven, Jr., *The Concept of the Public Forum,* 1965 SUP. CT. REV. 1, 23–25.

13. *See* Robert C. Post, *Meiklejohn's Mistake: Individual Autonomy and the Reform of Public Discourse,* 64 U. COLO. L. REV. 1109, 1113–19 (1993), *reprinted in* ROBERT C. POST, CONSTITUTIONAL DOMAINS: DEMOCRACY, COMMUNITY, MANAGEMENT 268 (1995). For a penetrating criticism of Post, *see also* Morris Lipson, *Autonomy and Democracy,* 104 YALE L.J. 2249.

14. *See generally* KALVEN, *supra* note 10, at 3–236.

15. *See, e.g.,* Katzenbach v. Morgan, 384 U.S. 641, 653 (1966).

Chapter 7

1. New York Times Co. v. United States, 403 U.S. 713, 725 (1971). *See generally* John Cary Sims, *Triangulating the Boundaries of Pentagon Papers,* 2 WM. & MARY BILL RTS. J. 341 (1993).

2. 403 U.S. at 726–27.

3. 403 U.S. at 730.

4. 403 U.S. at 733.

5. Pittsburgh Press Co. v. Pittsburgh Comm'n on Human Relations, 413 U.S. 376, 396 (1973) (dissenting opinion). The pressure for a prompt decision in the Pentagon Papers case required independent writing by the Justices, without the usual circulation and consultation among them. The traditional process often brings out the common elements and sharpens the points of disagreement.

6. Org. for a Better Austin v. Keefe, 402 U.S. 415 (1971).

7. 283 U.S. 697, 716 (1931).

8. 427 U.S. 539 (1976).

9. The test is from United States v. Dennis, 183 F.2d 201, 212 (2d Cir. 1950), *aff'd* 341 U.S. 494 (1951). It is quoted and adopted in *Nebraska Press,* 427 U.S. at 562.

10. 427 U.S. at 563.

11. Both the result in *Nebraska Press* and the method of analysis, in effect creating a strong presumption against gag orders, tend to impeach the laxity of the verbal formula, the use of the discounted "clear and present danger" test as the prior restraint standard. On the other hand, the fears of Justices Brennan and Stewart are not unfounded: (a) A verbal formula often develops an independent life of its own, apart from its application to a set of facts in a particular case. (b) The Justices might have feared that the verbal formula would not be likely to produce as congenial results in domains such as national security, where the "evil" is so "grave" and the alternative means of control not as obvious, as in a trial. (c) The verbal formula might have been seen by Brennan and Stewart as having disturbing implications for the subsequent restraint standard. If the discounted "clear and present danger" standard is the standard for prior restraints, and that is supposed to be the higher standard, one could only wonder—or fear—what the standard might be for subsequent restraints: Might it be the rationality standard of the World War I cases, which held that censorship would be justified if the criminal statute bears some reasonable relationship to the perceived threat to legitimate state interests?

12. It was Justice White's irresoluteness on this issue, I suspect, that accounts for the gap in the Per Curiam opinion as to the stringency of the standard for prior restraint: His vote—the fifth—was needed to achieve majority status for the Per Curiam.

13. The structural similarity between injunctions and criminal statutes is explored more fully in my book: OWEN M. FISS, THE CIVIL RIGHTS INJUNCTION (1978). For a similar perspective, *see* Stephen R. Barnett, *The Puzzle of Prior Restraint,* 29 STAN L. REV. 539 (1977).

14. These and other differences between injunctions and criminal statutes, and their relevance for the prior restraint doctrine, are discussed in more detail in FISS, *supra* note 14, at 69–74.

15. *See infra* note 18 and accompanying text for possible explanations for a response that otherwise remains inexplicable.

16. *See* Vance v. Universal Amusement Co. Inc., 445 U.S. 308 (1980); Pittsburgh Press Co. v. Pittsburgh Comm'n on Human Relations, 413 U.S. 976 (1973); Org. for a Better Austin v. Keefe, 402 U.S. 415 (1971). As the Court moved to the Right during the 1980s and 1990s, the strategic importance of the prior restraint doctrine diminished, as did its use. *See, e.g.,* Madsen v. Women's Health Center, 114 S. Ct. 2516 (1994) (declining to apply prior restraint analysis to injunction barring protests); Alexander v. United States, 113 S. Ct. 2766 (1993) (declining to apply prior restraint analysis to confiscation of materials not known to be obscene).

17. I suspect that the *Times*'s divided response to the Attorney General's telegram might be profitably analyzed from this perspective, too. The promise to obey the injunction might on this account be seen not as evidence of the injunction's greater force, but as a bargaining ploy, a way of inducing the Attorney General not to prosecute the *Times* under the Espionage Act but rather to proceed by seeking an injunction.

Chapter 8

1. *See* RFE/RL Research Institute Staff, *Regional Survey: The Media in Eastern Europe,* RADIO FREE EUROPE/RADIO LIBERTY RES. REP. 22, 22–23, 26, 28, 29, 31, 32 (May 7, 1993).

2. For a discussion of the various ways in which the state may interfere with the free functioning of the press, see HARRY KALVEN, JR., A WORTHY TRADITION: FREEDOM OF SPEECH IN AMERICA 3–73 (1988).

3. New York Times Co. v. Sullivan, 376 U.S. 254, 272 (1964).

4. Although the democracies emerging in the former Soviet empire continue to struggle in carving out an independent role for their judiciaries, on specific occasions the Russian and Hungarian Constitutional Courts have lent a measure of protection to the press and have kept hostile government officials at bay. *See* Frances H. Foster, *Izvestiia as a Mirror of Russian Legal Reform: Press, Law, and Crisis in the Post-Soviet Era,* 26 VAND. J. TRANSNAT'L L. 675, 694–702 (1993); Andrew Arato, The Hungarian Constitutional Court in the Media War: Interpretations of Division of Power and Model of Democracy 4–5 (June 21, 1993) (paper presented at Central European University conference "The Development of Rights of Access to the Media").

5. *See* Bill Carter, *Few Sponsors for TV War News,* N.Y. TIMES, Feb. 7, 1991, at D1, col. 3; Rick DuBrow, *TV and the Gulf Wars: TV Networks Shying from Vivid Violence,* L.A. TIMES, Feb. 7, 1991, at A10, col. 5. In response to the withdrawal of advertiser support,

CBS executives assured advertisers that "war specials could be tailored to provide better lead-ins to commercials. One way would be to insert the commercials after segments that were specially produced with upbeat images or messages about the war, like patriotic views from the home front." Carter, *supra*.

6. Writing on the Polish experience, Karol Jakubowicz makes a similar distinction between what he terms "free communication" and "democratic communication." He argues that the emerging democracies of Central and Eastern Europe have placed greater emphasis on the libertarian, market-oriented concept of "free communication" than on communication that is representative of the community at large. *See* Karol Jakubowicz, *Freedom vs. Equality,* 1993 E. EUR. CONST. REV. 42, 43.

7. New York Times v. Sullivan, 376 U.S. at 270.

8. *Cf.* Akhil R. Amar, *The Bill of Rights as a Constitution,* 100 YALE L.J. 1131, 1147–52 (1991) (challenging conventional wisdom that First Amendment freedoms of speech and press are essentially aimed at protecting minorities and arguing that "structural core" of First Amendment seeks to protect popular majorities from hostile congressional action).

9. U.S. CONST. amend. I.

10. A MAGYAR KÖZTÁRSASÁG ALKETMÁNYA [Constitution] ch. XII, §[nbs]61, cl. 2 (Hungary).

11. *See, e.g.,* Robert H. Bork, *Neutral Principles and Some First Amendment Problems,* 47 IND. L.J. 1 (1971).

12. *See* Vincent Blasi, *The Checking Value in First Amendment Theory,* 1977 AM. B. FOUND. RES. J. 523.

13. For a discussion of the ways in which the Western press has failed to cover the "grand issues," including social structure and distribution of wealth, see CHARLES E. LINDBLOM, POLITICS AND MARKETS: THE WORLD'S POLITICAL-ECONOMIC SYSTEMS 204–07 (1977).

14. *See* Charles Fried, *The New First Amendment Jurisprudence: A Threat to Liberty,* 59 U. CHI. L. REV. 225, 235–37 (1992).

15. For a discussion of the background and content of the fairness doctrine, see Red Lion Broadcasting v. FCC, 395 U.S. 367, 369–71 (1969). *See also* Randall Rainey, *The Public's Interest in Public Affairs Discourse, Democratic Governance, and Fairness in Broadcasting: A Critical Review of the Public Interest Duties of the Electronic Media,* 82 GEO. L.J. 269 (1993).

16. *See* Miami Herald Publishing Co. v. Tornillo, 418 U.S. 241 (1974).

17. *See* Columbia Broadcasting Sys. v. FCC, 453 U.S. 367 (1981).

18. *See* Columbia Broadcasting Sys. v. Democratic Nat'l Comm., 412 U.S. 94 (1973).

19. Despite antitrust laws and enforcement in the United States, 98% of all American cities with a daily newspaper had only one such publication as of 1986. *See* Robbie Steel, *Joint Operating Agreements in the Newspaper Industry: A Threat to First Amendment Freedoms,* 138 U. PA. L. REV. 275, 277 (1989). *See generally* William E. Lee, *Antitrust Enforcement, Freedom of the Press, and the "Open Market": The Supreme Court on the Structure and Content of Mass Media,* 32 VAND. L. REV. 1249 (1979).

20. *See* Second Report and Order, Amendment to Rules Relating to Multiple Ownership of Standard, FM, and Television Stations, 50 F.C.C.2d 1046 (1975). The FCC's "cross-ownership" rules were at issue in 1988 in the Court of Appeals for the District of Columbia. *See* News America Publishing v. FCC, 844 F.2d 800 (D.C. Cir. 1988).

21. *See* Public Broadcasting Act, 47 U.S.C. §§ 390–99 (1967).

22. CARNEGIE COMMISSION ON EDUCATIONAL TELEVISION, PUBLIC TELEVISION: A PROGRAM FOR ACTION (1967).

23. The United States Supreme Court upheld the constitutionality of this policy in *Metro Broadcasting, Inc. v. FCC,* 497 U.S. 547 (1990). Two years later, however, the United States Court of Appeals for the D.C. Circuit invalidated a similar FCC policy giving preference to women in the licensing process. *See* Lamprecht v. FCC, 958 F.2d 382 (D.C. Cir. 1992). The author of *Lamprecht,* Clarence Thomas, is now a Justice of the Supreme Court. Four of the five Justices in the majority in *Metro Broadcasting,* Justices Brennan, White, Marshall, and Blackmun, have since retired.

24. *See* Miami Herald Publishing Co v. Tornillo, 418 U.S. 241, 242 (1974).

25. *See* Turner Broadcasting System, Inc. v. FCC, 114 S. Ct. 2445 (1994) (holding that must-carry provisions, because of special burdens and obligations they impose upon cable operators, demand heightened but not the strictest First Amendment scrutiny).

26. The Supreme Court has recognized the place of television and radio as part of the working press in other areas of the law, such as libel, where broadcasters are endowed with the very same privileges and responsibilities that belong to newspapers. Admittedly, the obscenity standard has been adjusted to permit greater state control of the electronic media. *See* FCC v. Pacifica Found. 438 U.S. 726 (1978). Nevertheless, this greater state control is premised on the difficulty of shielding unwitting or especially vulnerable audiences (e.g., children) from radio or television broadcasts, rather than on the idea that television or radio are not part of the press.

27. Jerome A. Barron, *Access to the Press—A New First Amendment Right,* 80 HARV. L. REV. 1641 (1967). Professor Barron further developed his ideas in JEROME A. BARRON, FREEDOM OF THE PRESS FOR WHOM? THE RIGHT OF ACCESS TO MASS MEDIA (1973).

28. Fried, *supra* note 14, at 253. Fried applied this metaphor to all program regulation, which he refers to as "forced programming," on the questionable hypothesis that the public will always tune out.

29. *See* T.M. Scanlon, Jr., *Content Regulation Reconsidered, in* DEMOCRACY AND THE MASS MEDIA 331 (Judith Lichtenberg ed., 1990); Geoffrey R. Stone, *Content-Neutral Restrictions,* 54 U. CHI. L. REV. 46 (1987). *See generally* KALVEN, *supra* note 2.

30. By statute, the Corporation for Public Broadcasting is largely independent of control by Congress or the executive; 47 U.S.C. § 398(a) (1994) prohibits "any department, agency, officer, or employee of the United States [from exercising] any direction, supervision, or control over public telecommunications, or over the Corporation or any of its grantees or contractors, or over the charter or bylaws of the Corporation. . . ." Measures have also been taken to lessen the influence of partisan politics on the Corporation. The members of the Corporation's board are appointed by the President and confirmed by the Senate, but 47 U.S.C. § 396(c)(1) (1994) provides that no more than six of the ten members may be from the same political party. *See generally* Steven D. Zansberg, *"Objectivity and Balance" in Public Broadcasting: Unwise, Unworkable, and Unconstitutional,* 12 YALE L. & POL'Y REV. 184 (1994) (arguing that 1992 "objectivity and balance" amendment to legislation reauthorizing funding for Corporation for Public Broadcasting is unconstitutional and inconsistent with purpose of government-funded public broadcasting).

31. 319 U.S. 624 (1943).

32. *Id.* at 629.

33. 475 U.S. 1 (1986).

34. Syracuse Peace Council, 2 F.C.C.R. 5043, 5057, 5070 n.227, 5071 nn.241–46 (1987), *aff'd,* 867 F.2d 654 (D.Cir. 1989).

35. PruneYard Shopping Center v. Robins, 447 U.S. 74 (1980).

36. *Pacific Gas,* 475 U.S. at 19.

Acknowledgments

Since the mid-1980s I have offered a free speech course at the Yale Law School. Almost all the essays in this volume have evolved from the passionate debates that occurred in that course, and I wish to thank the many, many students who participated in them—those who egged me on as well as those who fiercely resisted. Two of those students—Andrew L. Shapiro and Olivier S. Sultan, both of the class of 1995—first conceived of this collection and were primarily responsible for putting it all together. I am enormously grateful to them, not just for their intelligence and good will but also for the joyful hours we spent working together. This book and the essays in it also benefited from views and efforts of a great number of colleagues, friends, assistants, and editors: Bruce Ackerman, Amy M. Adler, Akhil Reed Amar, Jennifer K. Brown, Patricia L. Cheng, Sunny Yao-Chung Chu, Joshua Cohen, Gadi Dechter, Elizabeth E. deGrazia, Charles Fried, Mark K. Friedman, Gayton P. Gomez, Matthew S. Haiken, Donald W. Hawthorne, Daniel G. Hildebrand, Jamie Kalven, Alvin K. Klevorick, Christopher Kutz, Catharine A. MacKinnon, Burke Marshall, Frank I. Michelman, Nina T. Pirrotti, Robert C. Post, Monroe E. Price, George L. Priest, Richard C. St. John, Thomas Scanlon, Reva B. Siegel, Robert James Slaughter, David F. Solomon, Anne P. Standley, Martin J. Stone, and Cass R. Sunstein. Glancing at the circle that surrounds me, I feel blessed. On that note let me once again single out my secretary, Lorraine E. Nagle, for her extraordinary contribution to this volume and my work in general. She is responsible for much of the esprit that engulfs us all.

Owen M. Fiss

About the Author

Owen M. Fiss is Sterling Professor of Law at Yale University. He was educated at Dartmouth (1959), Oxford (1961), and Harvard Law School (1964). He clerked for Thurgood Marshall during the 1964–1965 term of court, when Marshall was a judge of the United States Court of Appeals for the Second Circuit, and for Justice William J. Brennan, Jr., during the 1965–1966 term. Following these clerkships Fiss served in the Civil Rights Division of the Department of Justice and, before moving to Yale, taught at the University of Chicago.

Index